Christians and the
World of Computers

D0219453

BR
115
.C65
R65
1990

Christians
and the
World of Computers

*Professional and Social Excellence
in the Computer World*

Parker Rossman and
Richard Kirby

SCM PRESS
London

TRINITY PRESS INTERNATIONAL
Philadelphia

WITHDRAWN

HIEBERT LIBRARY 34005
Fresno Pacific College - M. B. Seminary
Fresno, Calif 93702

This edition first published 1990

SCM Press Ltd
26–30 Tottenham Road
London N1 4BZ

Trinity Press International
3725 Chestnut Street
Philadelphia PA 19104

All rights reserved. No part of this publication may be
reproduced, stored in a retrieval system, or transmitted,
in any form or by any means, electronic, mechanical,
photocopying, recording or otherwise, without the prior
written permission of the publishers, SCM Press Ltd and Trinity
Press International.

© Parker Rossman and Richard Kirby 1990

British Library Cataloguing in Publication Data

Rossman, Parker
Christians and the world of computers.
1. Computer sciences. Christian viewpoints
I. Title   II. Kirby, Richard
261.56

ISBN 0–334–02468–4

Library of Congress Cataloging-in-Publication Data

Rossman, Parker.
Christians and the world of computers / Parker Rossman,
Richard Kirby.
p.   cm.
Includes bibliographical references.
ISBN 0–334–02468–4
1. Computers—Religious aspects—Christianity.   I. Kirby,
Richard, 1949–   . II. Title.
BR115.C85R65   1990
261.5'6—dc20   90–41636

Typeset at The Spartan Press Ltd, Lymington, Hants
Printed in England by
Clays Ltd, St Ives plc

Contents

Preface

You and nearly all people are already involved with computers, not only in your cars and microwave ovens, but also – perhaps against your will – in your medical, insurance, and income tax records and much more. All of us increasingly live in this "milieu of computers," and all Christians have a stake in helping define our responsibility and calling in that inescapable milieu which shapes our futures more than we know.

This book is for those who seek to initiate a Christian response to and responsible recognition of involvement in the area of "information age technology" and its claims.

When we speak of the "computer world" – with a *Christian* call to vocational and social excellence – we distinguish and address ourselves to three categories of personnel. Many of them are imagining – and seeking to create – astonishing futures for computers and computer-empowered tools:

computer professionals (students and teachers of computer science; inventors and imaginers, even hackers; engineers and electronic technologists; manufacturers, retailers, programmers and other entrepreneurs, computer journalists and the staff of professional computer associations);

school-teachers, computer users at home and at work, including *church-related workers who are involved with computers* (youth workers, members of congregations and communities of Christians, pastors, bishops and executives, missionaries and missiologists, theologians and teachers, monks, nuns and members of orders);

social critics of both religion and computer science of four types: futurists, including religious futurists; social philosophers such as McLuhan; science fiction writers; artists who are imagining the future and often influencing it more than they intend or realize.

We suggest concepts of moral and professional excellence for each of these groupings with some guidelines for cumulatively developing ethical codes.

We intend this to be a study book, both for individuals and group study, not to answer questions so much as to begin to ask questions that have not been adequately addressed in a Christian context. The book has nine segments which we call "chapters," but these segments can be presented by teachers or pastors as modules in a nine-session learning experience. The order is not fixed, and we would encourage leaders to experiment with the most effective sequence.

We intend a special word of encouragement to youth workers and to teenage and university student readers. They are most likely to be the ones who feel a special kinship with what is said here. Many young people already have a great interest and involvement in computers, and they have the idealism and energy to undertake the creative and empowering tasks proposed here. Church leaders should therefore be encouraged to organize conferences of young people and youth leaders of the upcoming generation on these issues.

The book begins with a survey of the frontiers of computer science and technology within a Christian perspective. We ask where computers – including computer science, related supercomputer tools, programming, etc. – are going. For example, we point to the fact that they are being used in space travel, in robotics, in military systems, in brain research, as the "central nervous system" of an emerging "world brain" of interrelated data bases. Some scientists even believe that computers are becoming or should become persons. We ask then if these directions in computer science – some of them very worrysome – are inevitable in the providence of God.

As Christians, we assert that "it does not have to be this way," that this exploitative phase of science is simply one possible track in human history. It is one which has resulted from society's moral choices as much as from its "scientific research." Different moral choices can produce a different computer science moving in alternative directions. Christ, we assert in the third chapter, not only reveals God's moral value structure, but also sends the Holy Spirit *to build a new scientific community*. In this perspective, we can see where computers *should* be going: to empower action for the hungry, the imprisoned, the sick; and to the places where bureaucratic logjams and information chaos need to be unraveled.

Donald Straus, for example, proposed to the Columbia University faculty seminar on "Computers, People, and Society" that existing research tools have largely empowered specialization. Yet society's emerging crises, such as ecological and environmental pollution, require new software to enable interdisciplinary, international, and collective research and action: teamwork to bring many minds together to solve problems that are beyond the scope of any one mind alone, even the greatest genius.

So in the fourth chapter we take a look at computers planned and deployed for compassionate purposes. Examples include networking of agencies and researchers (such as those working to feed hungry children) and stimulating creativity, global networks for peace, the global electronic consortium of universities, and other adventurous possibilities in education.

In chapter five we address motivation – how to get computer people to act to solve global problems – in "The Christian Mission to Those Involved with Computers" by discussing principles for Christian ministry to the world of computers in its ideas, its people, and its technology. The sixth chapter looks at the calling of those involved with computers which, we suggest, includes seeking the will of God, reflecting theologically on computer science, developing a shared Christian life style, and establishing linkages between economics and computer science, so that the poor can benefit. In chapter seven, then, we deal with vocational and social excellence.

Chapter eight asks, What is God doing in the information age? It discusses different attitudes that Christians take concerning technology as we explore the positive contribution of computer science toward the life of the church and the future development of compassionate theology. Then, in a concluding chapter, "Christian Life in the Information Age," we outline the beginning of what we hope can stimulate and point to some new directions for theology for the computer world, in which the "people of God" can engage in an urgent transfer of compassion to the world of computers and their users.

Each chapter has two parts, text and study materials. In each chapter the main argument is followed by short biographies, Bible study suggestions, and worship guidelines. In this way, our text is designed as a course text for a wide range of uses: for college, high school, university or continuing education courses in information technology, futures studies, religious studies –

and of course, theology and Christianity courses in school or parish.

London and New Haven
March 1990

Editor's note: Modified American spelling and punctuation is used in this book, although it was written and published jointly in the U.S.A. and England.

A Meditation for the Reader

The Holy Spirit is now making it possible for the world of computers to be given a new start. In this book, we show what form this new beginning can take. A basic starting point in our thinking is the fact that neither "science" nor "technology" is really "value free." The word "science" is an adaptation of the Latin word *scientia*, which simply means knowledge. There are many types and many theories of knowledge. Each of these theories is built upon ideas of ultimate value. We seek "knowledge" not of "truth" or "pure facts," but of things which engage our deepest values. Even the *idea* of knowledge or knowing contains earlier moral choices about ultimate reality.

The world of computers, which is less than a century old, has been built on a theory of knowledge whose values are economic, financial, and technological. A theory of knowledge built on Christian values of compassion, justice, and love can lead to an entirely different "computer science;" and a transformed computer milieu for human service.

In this book we try to show what God is doing in the world of computers and what this means for Christians. It is as if the Lord, the Holy Spirit, is inviting the people of God to join a festival of ethical, scientific creativity. We hope you will help lead the way into this new world so as to work with computers for compassionate purposes and to the greater glory of God.

Introduction: The Milieu

We write this for all who are influenced by the "computer world" – which is nearly everyone in Western society these days – and for those who work in that milieu. We use the term "computer world" to include all who create, manufacture, sell, use professionally, repair, and provide services to those who use computers; and also the amateurs, the hackers, game-players, home computer users, and other amateurs who are involved in the "world of computers" (all of us more than we realize).

We also ask vocational questions about a third group of people: writers, futurists, teachers, artists and musicians (computer-created art and music), small-business folk, clergy, and politicians who are entering this "computer world" (sometimes against their will).

Many of these people are church members who have given little thought to their calling in this "world" which God loves and where they are called to witness and serve. So we need to define the Christian calling in this milieu.

In this world are many computer societies and "users groups" which seek to "serve." Their purposes tend to be to maximize efficiency; to promote profitable enterprises (and find ways to save money); to share expertise; to develop standards for manufacturers, teachers, business firms that use them, and students.

Until recently, questions about God in relation to computers have been given two types of answers: one is that computers are essentially diabolical (as Jacques Ellul on technology), and so are not God's at all but are part of enemy action.

The other answer has been that computers pose no issues or new possibilities for theology any more than do adding machines and typewriters. Within such a response, it is assumed that computers in themselves reveal or express nothing new about God or God's people. Furthermore, it is assumed that even the use of computers by theologians implies zero advancement in either the method or content of theology. One theologian, hearing about hypertext/CI theological-journal ideas, said rather condescendingly, "It is a pity it won't tell us anything new about *God*!"

Another said: "In my remaining years I must complete what I started and leave it to younger theologians to think about such technology."

A third theologian said that computers have no contribution to make to religious research; they can only distract theologians and their students from the proper subject matter of theology, which is the primordial revelation and the dogmas of the patristic period. Theological work, he said, is the clarification of the primal Christian dogmas. He saw no point of intersection between this essentially faith-oriented, prayer-governed spiritual activity and the mechanical methods and ambitions of the computer world.

A fourth theologian said: "The danger of computers is that they substitute speed and depersonalized efficiency for faith and integrity as spiritual ideals."

Such theologians are often centering their theology on a particular concept of "revelation." They believe that in ancient times God revealed to us all that human beings need to know. Meanwhile, and this is a quintessential dogma of their theology, nothing new can take place in either revelation or theology. This is a very central axiom for some theologians. For them, theology is changeless, where science grows and changes. Theology is the anchor, maybe science is the sails. But in their view the ship of revelation simply cannot change, because if God is changeless, theology certainly must be!

However, this is not the only view of revelation. Let us consider a different starting point, a Christian view that God's self-revelation in Christ Jesus is not the *end* but a *beginning* of revelation (John 14:12: "Greater things than I do, you shall do"). More truth is to unfold as human beings pray and study the Bible and seek to discern God's presence in the world today; God has more of her/himself to reveal, to share with us.

The "Christ-event" (the life, death, and resurrection of Jesus) was thus not the end of revelation, but the commencement of a new period of salvation history (Berdyaev's "age of the Spirit"). The people of God can experience continuing revelation if they faithfully live in the power of the Holy Spirit.

Berdyaev is among those Christians who see God as actively present in our co-creation, in human creativity, in the unfolding of the Spirit in all areas of community and life.

As many futurists realize, we live in an era when change rather than stasis is the central feature of the human community. Is this change, whether good or evil, to be regarded as irrelevant to theology and unrelated to God's action in the world? To say so is unwittingly to subscribe to heresies, such as the idea that the real world is merely an illusion; or the idea that God is dead or no longer has anything to do with us. This, however, is not the Christian position. God is not dead. The living God is present in creation and in partnership with people.

Theologians thus find themselves on the horns of a dilemma as they contemplate the world of computer science.

On the one hand, it seems that they must say that all these changes, the new bursts of creativity, are irrelevant to theology. On the other hand, if they admit that the changes really do matter and are theologically relevant, then they must do some fundamentally new thinking about God's ceaseless activity in relation to the reality of ongoing creation. If it is conceded that God's own Spirit might be present in computer science, it is necessary to ask what, theologically, is happening.

We invite the reader to join us in a journey of exploration, to enter the world of the computer, to consider its moral meaning and destiny . . . from God's point of view. We begin therefore by asking, Where in the world (and beyond) are computers going?!

1

Where Are Computers Going?

Does it matter where computers are going, their future direction?

It does if you are interested in where the human race – all men, women, and children – are going in a time when humanity is at risk.

It matters if you are curious and concerned about the apparently endless growth of the power and scope of science and technology – and their potential for good or evil.

It especially matters when you realize that science, including computer science, is the outcome of human investigation, invention, and choice – and the same applies to the future of computers and related technology.

The future of computers – where they and the human race are going – is determined by our thoughts, prayers, choices, and decisions.

All of us who are concerned about our future, and especially those who wish to play a part in the future of computer science, need to spend time finding out what kind of future is being planned for computers. We need to learn how the advocates of ever-greater computer science see such a future as relating to human nature, human need, and human social-political institutions.

To try to find out where computers are going is a way, also, to explore human nature itself – its future and the future of all the sciences. Looking at the directions of computer technology can be a good way to engage the frontiers of thought of the greatest contemporary philosophers. It can lead us to discover what planet earth's leading thinkers, scientists, and futurists think about the direction of human and scientific evolution, development, progress, and growth.

In ancient times, the nations equipped their societies with soothsayers, shamans, prophets, seers, mystics, and ecstatics to "read the signs of the times," to interpret to the society where it was going. This kind of social role was always a mixture of several elements: where society and its members were actually going (a prediction on the basis of the best available evidence), and where people *should be going* (what moral values or ethical justice requires). In the Jewish scriptures, Isaiah 40 is an example of a rich combination of these elements, of what the prophet saw being revealed by God, nature, and human events. During a thousand-year period in the life and culture of the Hebrews, this prophetic task had two elements: *foretelling*, or predicting; and *forthtelling*, or announcing the needed guidance/judgment, declaring the "word of the Lord" glimpsed by the seer or heard by the prophet.

In our late twentieth century, this kind of seership is rather uneasily distributed among scientists and science fiction writers, philosophers and the planning branches of national governments, futurists and theologians, psychologists and mystics. The World Network of Religious Futurists is now endeavoring to make a coherent pattern out of this slight confusion of roles and skills. Even among *futurists* there is a surprising range of different types.[1] Alvin Toffler, the author of *Future Shock* and *The Third Wave*, is not John Naisbitt who predicts the future for business; and neither is much like H. G. Wells who dreamed of science creating an ideal world, or Herman Kahn who was optimistic about science solving the major problems of human society. Similarly, *religious* futurists exhibit an as-yet-unclassified range of differences among themselves in gifts, interests, scientific outlook, and values.

How can any of them know where computers are going?

We can find out by studying trends and "descriptive statistics" which are published, for example, in learned journals, in abstracts and books, with reference to science, technology, engineering, education, and government, war and space travel. We can read the articles on the philosophy of computer science written by its enthusiasts. These enthusiasts often include computer scientists and engineers, teachers and science journalists, entrepreneurs and industrialists, futurists, philosophers of science, science fiction writers, and the bureaucratic leaders of computer-user societies and their publications.

Even astronomers and geneticists find that they cannot understand the meaning of their own subject and the directions of their research without some speculation about the direction of computer science and computers.

Yet much of what futurists write is speculation and only speculation. It takes a lot of skill to sort out science fiction from speculation, prophecy, prediction, fantasy, and hope as we study the sometimes extravagant writings about the future of computer science. This is one reason why futurists seek to develop a system of classification of pictures of the future. A quite well-known one is the distinction between the "3 P's;" possible, probable, and preferable futures.

Possible, Probable, or Preferable?

Futurists have classified visions and plans as being one of three kinds of "future."

Probable futures (let's call them P1) are those which are very likely to occur. For example, there most probably will be many schools in 1995 in which every child has a computer.

Possible futures (P2) are ones about which we can only speculate. It is *possible* that nuclear fusion, combined with computer technology, will produce limitless free energy by the year 2020.

Preferable futures (P3) are those which we judge to be desirable in terms of our values. This can help us to distinguish from among many possible future tracks of our culture, and to place our energies in activities which will more likely result in the kind of future we want. For example, if we want robotics for the military-industrial complex – or want to create robots to replace humane persons – we place our investments there. If we prefer robotics to be developed to help handicapped persons, we will invest in a different kind of science.

So we invite you, our readers, to think about each of the directions of computer science and classify each one as possible (P1), probable (P2), or preferable (P3).

Well, where are computers going?

Some of the possible directions, elaborated from current uses or discovered or proposed by scientists or futurist-scholars – some not carefully examined – may surprise you! One prophetic voice in the computer world, whose predictions across two decades have more often come true than not, is Theodor "Ted" Nelson, author of *Computer Lib/ Dream Machines*.[2] He worries about a "computer priesthood," experts who make things unnecessarily complicated to keep others dependent on them. He worries, for example, about computers continuing to go down a careless and sloppy path which frustrates creativity by solidifying in computer hardware the wrong ways of doing things.

Going To the Stars!

Adrian Berry, science journalist and futurist,[3] often writes of the astronomical future of the human species. Following the philosophical vision of astronomers Barrow and Tipler,[4] he asserts that "any advanced civilization would inevitably have discovered the secret of interstellar travel." He agrees with them that this secret lies not in "ultra-fast spaceships" but in "*ultrasophisticated computing machines.*" Tipler himself believes that "it is a deficiency in computer technology, not in rocket technology, which prevents us from beginning the exploration of the galaxy tomorrow."

Berry recalls that in 1948 the Hungarian-born scientist, John von Neumann, wrote the blueprint for "a startling new kind of computer" which could be built within the next few decades. It could, he proposed, make things, anything, even identical copies of itself. Later scientists call these "von Neumann machines." It is this kind of computer which, the vision goes, could be "going to the stars." Computers, of course, are already on the unmanned space vehicles which are exploring distant planets.

"Using von Neumann machines," Adrian Berry[5] suggests, "A civilization could colonize our entire galaxy of 150,000 suns in a few million years, in the same way the far-flung Pacific Islands were colonized: first a single expedition would settle an island. A dozen more expeditions would set out from this island in turn. Thus it went on, enabling the settlement of tens of thousands of habitable islands by what had begun as a single expedition."

In Berry's vision, the same thing could happen in space if humans set out to colonize an empty universe. But computers would go first, traveling ahead of us from star to star. Being so much more durable and long-lived than we, the computers would outlast us. With our extinction, the cosmos would still be ruled by descendants, or at least the creations, of humanity. "They could prolong the life of the universe almost indefinitely. They could become as mighty as the galaxies which compose it and they could prevent their collapse into an ultimate black hole in which matter, space, and time would otherwise be extinguished."

Whatever the scientific merits of that vision, it reveals a strange feature of the "psychology of many scientists:" the widespread idea that unconscious – and insensitive, even inhumane – machines are the true successors of humankind in the "evolutionary process."[6]

A psychoanalyst might respond along the following lines: Human nature is messy and painful, and scientists in particular often seem attracted by logic, math, and machinery because these seem to provide an escape from painful and deep feelings, from emotional confusion, and perhaps from the plight of the human family, the pain and sorrow of the world's millions of sick and hungry children.

It is therefore logical to extend this vision into the future of the human race as a whole. To believe that we are destined to be superseded by machines, devoid of feelings and therefore of both pain and irrationality, is in this view a "consummation devoutly to be wished." Such a wish is, however, unacceptable to society and to most persons in society, and is therefore first repressed (denied) and then projected (distanced from self) onto the "external world." It is then considered to be a part of "the universe" (ultimate reality), and it becomes natural first to imagine, then to believe, then to prophesy that such an "evolutionary victory of machines" is not only natural but desirable. Almost the last stage in this psychological process is to campaign for public funds to be used for creating such machines; and the last stage is for such scientists and their disciples to create a philosophy of life and death which exalts the machine and proposes it as the "natural" successor of humanity.

In such a milieu of thought it is logical enough to propose that computers or robots are actually "persons" and should be recognized legally as such. Many current films entertain us with such "human" robots and enlarge such myths about computers. The illogicality of seeing mindless automata as "representatives" of human beings is easily forgotten, and the vision of a universe altogether devoid of human consciousness and compassion becomes balm for the pain and growth which consciousness and its attendant feelings (and love) brings.

> Perhaps we can see something here that is comparable to the way that Laurens van der Post, the Jungian philosopher and historian of culture, points out the irony of the use of decapitation in the French revolution. Humanity is not going to get rid of its head or intellect – it obstinately remains! Neither, unfortunately, will the heart (feelings) go away – whether in the Fascist-neo-Nietzschean vision of the Übermensch or superman, or in the cool, painless computer machine.

The psychoanalysis of computer science as a cultural phenomenon is only now coming to birth as a branch of psychological enquiry.[7] Almost everything remains to be done in investigating the causes – and the remedy (therapy, treatment) – for this "split" in the human psyche. It is an "alienation" by humanity from its own deepest feelings and from the pain of its own hurts, from its degradation and endemic self-inflicted torment. But as psychology pursues a systematic inquiry into "the world of computers," there is real hope that the alienation can be healed, the split in the psyche overcome, and a more compassionate use of human energies undertaken. As this cultural healing process gets underway, alternative visions of "the universe" will arise.

This book seeks one such vision.

The analysis of the collective psyche of humanity and its science is not just a matter for psychologists. In earlier times, it was prophets who analyzed the collective mind and suggested a cure. In Sikhism, the Guru is sometimes described as the "Preceptor of Mankind." In Judaism, we recall the prophet Isaiah who announced the gift of healing in God's name and strove for a new synthesis of the contents of the psyche of the ancient Hebrews. He – and later Ezekiel – brought comfort to the battered psyche of the Israelites. Today's religious futurists may also be a species of "psycho-analyst" in this sense, as they endeavor to discern the path forward toward healing – for the collective psyche of humanity and for the culture and science of the human race.

Psychologists have identified the idea of the "shadow" or "unaccept-able" and therefore repressed side of human personality/psyche. But the whole human race has such a shadow (in mystical thought, the "Dweller on the Threshold"). Part of it is the intuitive sense of universal respons-ibility for all starving and tormented persons in all parts of the world.

Racing away from earth, scene of human misery and failures, escaping to the stars, is a natural attempt by the conscious personal mind to escape from this most unwelcome shadow. Unfortunately, it cannot be left behind on earth, but comes along too. It must be dealt with here, otherwise there will be no happiness among the stars either. Computers cannot erase the shadow, only moral and emotional growth can.[8]

Computers will go to the stars, but will it be for "star wars," the vision of "war forever" which is seen in so much science fiction? Or can they go to the stars in search of resources to bring a richer and more abundant life to all creatures?

Unto the Sixth Generation (of Computers)

Where are computers going? To their own future. Computers move ahead from "generation" to generation, that is, from room-sized com-puters that used vacuum tubes to file-cabinet-sized computers with transistors; to desktop computers with integrated circuits; to computers in all kinds of tools that use powerful fingernail-sized chips; to parallel processors and "neural" networking.

For an analogy of this growth and computer development in lay terms, we might compare these generations of computers to transportation: the first generation would be walking; second generation, riding a horse;

third generation, riding in an automobile; fourth generation, flying in an airplane; and the next generations, traveling on space ships.

These next generations of computers, as the previous ones, seek more and more *power* for users, for ordinary people. This power, sought in the name of economic growth and scientific progress, is a cluster of qualities including speed, magnitude, multi-dimensionality, and capacity. To some extent the qualities themselves are being sought after because they create a sense of awe.

Sixth generation computers[9] will be machines that learn, that speak and recognize human speech, that translate from one language to another, that "are influenced by the style of the brain," that engage in "cooperative communication" as "problem solving networks" and combinations of powerful instruments, and can easily be operated by gesture or word of mouth.

Alan Kay, inventor of the idea of a personal computer to empower all of us, says that the next stage of computer science will engage both left brain and right brain and all three kinds of human thinking: cognitive, imaging, and kinesthetic. The IBM PC is to him the model of an intellectual, word-manipulating machine; Apple's "Mac," with its windows and color graphics, is the imaging machine; and the computer chip in a helmet or suit, which the user operates by moving around, is the kinesthetic. Kay is inventing computerized environments in which school children move around, using their muscles to think, and more important to be better able to remember and use their knowledge and thinking abilities.

The rush ahead to create more and more powerful machines is also caused by the competitiveness between computer manufacturers and their sponsoring governments, including a military element. Although computer philosophers may declare that it is "inevitable" to go on to the seventh, eighth, to the nth generation, we ask if this investment of human energy and money has yet been morally justified in terms of basic human need. There is a self-perpetuating air about the construction of successive generations of computers. The fact is that they represent *cultural ideals*, projects, even toys (not forgetting that play is a component of creativity) for the human family as a whole; and until the moral destiny of the human race is clarified and alternative cultural ideals developed, the mystique of nth generation computers will remain.

There is nothing "inevitable" about this sequence, of more and more powerful military instruments of destruction, for example. To say that it is inevitable is simply to pretend that somebody else (e.g., God, nature, evolution) is making our choices. These choices follow from the pursuit of cultural ideals and from our understanding of reality. Different ideals and values will lead to different choices about the future of computers, and the feeling of "inevitability" about computer science would then vanish.

To Artificial Intelligence (A.I.)

Where else are computers going? Toward artificial intelligence. That is, some scientists assume it to be inevitable that computers will do more and more of our "thinking" for us – sooner or later doing "creative thinking" for human beings. Already there are successful computer programs which can assist physicians in medical diagnosis and which can explain and help others use the skills of experienced engineers. That machines will do our thinking for us is especially anticipated in areas of great complexity when decisions may be too much for the human mind; for example, computers may decide when to launch nuclear weapons.

Computer prophets like Ted Nelson also warn that human beings, who don't yet know how to think clearly enough with their minds, are not likely to build computer minds that are less fuzzy. At best they may be incompetent, at worst, evil. He warns that we should be "rightly uncertain and suspicious."

Artificial intelligence[10] is a *scientific and cultural ideal,* and like von Neumann machines, A.I. is not a fact, but an idea. The *idea* of A.I. is a cluster of cultural ambitions and beliefs wrapped up in a scientific and, more recently, a positive *mythic* form. There is a mystique about A.I., such that it easily becomes seen as an end in its own right. In some ways, this cultural ambition is a natural successor to the dream of Frankenstein's monster which Mary Shelley published in Victorian England. Would science allow humankind to play God, to imitate the Creator by *manufacturing life?*[11]

To create "artificially intelligent" machines is not, as some philosophers suppose, philosophical nonsense.[12] Rather, the effort is a natural attempt to extend the labor-saving power of machines into reasoning as well as the kind of brute force provided by pulleys and levers or bulldozers.

A.I. has not yet been achieved. But that is not the point. It remains a beguiling cultural ideal in pursuit of which human beings strive for self-knowledge and self-understanding. For by investigating A.I., we investigate the boundaries of personhood, the nature of intelligence, and the limits of the overlap between human being and machine. The study of these limits is one reason why the search for A.I. remains a cultural ideal supported by governments and scientific associations. There is even a playful dimension to A.I. research. By endeavoring to construct "intelligent machines," the human race unconsciously imagines it is flirting with danger – the danger of being superseded or "kept as pets." Innumerable science fiction stories portray such possibilities where the playful element of the imagined experimentation with power is clearly shown.[13]

The real philosophical question to ask A.I. researchers is not, Are you understanding or misunderstanding intelligence? The question should be, Does logic, reasoning, and problem-solving constitute the essence of personhood? Does A.I. *really* have anything to do with the imitation of persons – but rather with the imitation of depersonalized, alienated human beings – if it ignores the love, compassion, and the infinite resources of the spirit which are quintessentially human?

A.I. is a scientific idea which governs a program of research. It is a comparatively harmless idea, and rightly understood can be helpful to human moral progress. For it is a tool for the management of information in the same way that the wheel was used for the conveyance of goods and materials. So long as its limits as idea and ideal are understood, it can continue to inspire inventiveness and discovery in computer science.

Nevertheless, should not that inventiveness be directed toward human problems such as disease, famine, and preserving the ozone layer instead of toward war or wrongly imagined imitations of personhood? A.I. should not be a goal in itself, for such a goal would not only be philosophically but ethically incoherent.

Toward Personhood (Maybe?)

Where are computers going? Some scientists nevertheless expect computers to become persons. "The ultimate goal of A.I. research is to build a person."[14] One A.I. graduate student said: "To replicate personhood would be the 'Mount Everest' of computer research." Robert Jastrow, Professor of Astronomy at Columbia University, seems to be saying that computers represent the next stage of *human evolution*. Lawyers now begin to debate the civil rights and personhood of complex computers and of human-computer combinations. Jastrow also seems to say that if we want to build feelings into computers, "that's no problem."

In the assumption of some scientists that computers are going to become persons, there is not only moral but philosophical confusion. It is a "category mistake (error)," as philosophers say.[15] Must not the definition of "person" include its contradistinction from machines: the possession of consciousness, the capacity for love and spirituality, etc.? Are not some computer scientists confusing the possession of consciousness with the appearance – by engineered mimicry – of certain behavioral traits associated with persons? This is a truth which only love, the psychic sense, can grasp.

We have already analyzed some of the reasons *why* such a goal or destiny as this is supposed for computers. Psychologists can assure the followers of computer science that computers are *not* going toward personhood! They may go to the stars, we suggest, but will never (by definition) become persons.

Nor will persons ever become computers. The half-truth here is that persons may and will incorporate into their physical bodies some computerized organs. Yet this will no more make a person a computer than sitting in and driving a truck will make a person into a truck. Persons *use* – and cover themselves in – clothes and cars and maybe computers too. But this has no more significance for personhood than does the dressing up by which a six-year-old will "disguise" herself as a witch for trick-or-treating on Halloween. The neighbors still recognize her as a child, for she still exists! Computer-using persons are still persons – even in hyper-mechanical or technological disguise.

"Intelligent" or "smart" robots are coming as fast as budgets allow; probably along with cyborgs, androids, and exotic combinations of genetically engineered "alternative persons." Computer chips may be made of human brain matter, some scientists predict.

Computers, "merging" with robots, may result in "smart" (A.I.-type) robots, but they will not be people either, even if the robots are brilliant and are programmed to play dress-up and speak kind words. Psychologically speaking, robots satisfy a human need for servants, for undemanding partners and companions. In a world dominated by the idea that machines are real persons, it is understandable that some children should prefer robots to people. In a world where parents often leave their children to be raised by somebody else, or where they brutalize and exploit their children, we may not be surprised if children should even expect to be raised by computerized robots.

So we should reflect upon this: Is it true that computers are going into robots because the ways in which persons hurt each other have led to a desire for harmless people-substitutes? Isaac Asimov, forty years ago, formulated in science fiction the "law of robotics," rules to prevent robots from hurting human beings or from failing to protect them.

Robots may be called "Cyborgs" – we remember the television series "Six Million Dollar Man" – but a good disguise is still a disguise. A person with robotic appurtenances is still a person; a robot or cyborg-type robot dressed up as a person is still a robot. It is a spiritual and psychic truth that persons have soul; and the robot is no more a spiritual creature than urea synthesized in the laboratory is a spiritual creature.

Computers-in-robots enable us to play the game "Who am I?" better. So we expect much more computerized robotics, with grown-ups and children alike (led by teenagers) trying to fool one another by substituting robots for persons, that is, until we tire of the game. But society needs its games and jokers, as Arthur C. Clarke made a central element in his novel, *The City and the Stars*. Of course computers are increasingly inside all kinds of games.

Which, then, should be our priority? Robot warriors battling in space, or an expansion of the skills of robot servants who already enable some paralyzed persons to enter more fully into human life?

To the World Brain

Universities are heavily involved in all kinds of computer research and experimentation, especially in the creation of data bases and information-management systems. Here too, however, we ask where computers are going.

Ted Nelson worries about "information retrieval." Will machines be trusted to organize human knowledge and dispense it to us? Who will decide what goes into data bases or if all religion is categorized under "superstition?"

Computer software already makes it possible to collect in data bases, organize, sort out, and make available vast amounts of human information. However, Roszak asks us[16] if we are failing to distinguish between the true art of thinking and information processing by machine. Bureaucracies and the military-industrial complex require such vast amounts of data that only computers can provide it. But can computers ever help us understand the assumptions and values implicit in this data? Roszak worries about more than the inevitable inaccuracy of computer data bases (as we all see in the errors in our computerized bills). He worries about a "data processing model of the human mind."

If artificial intelligence will make it possible for computers to do our thinking for us, then are we to worry about the way computers are going into the creation of the "emerging world brain"? Rightly understood, this "world brain" is a bringing together of many human minds, authentic human reflection and intelligence, aided and empowered by combinations of new technology. For example, computers and computer networking are part of an emerging "global electronic encyclopedia," a synthesis and coding of all the world's knowledge, the interconnecting of all the world's research libraries and electronic data bases.

H. G. Wells promoted the "world brain" idea, perhaps influenced by Comenius, who tied the idea of a world encyclopedia – which would bring together and organize all the world's knowledge – with the concept to the idea of universal education and literacy. The computer-based "world brain" idea grows from the Universal Bibliographical Repertory – created to hold one copy of every printed book – and the International Federation for Documentation, UNESCO, and now electronic and computer developments. These make possible the electronic scanning, coding, word and idea indexing, putting on line, and interconnecting of hundreds of thousands of interconnected dispersed information systems, bringing together all the world's knowledge not unlike the way knowledge is stored in the human brain.

Computers and related technology in that system make it possible to include sound, films, and graphics so that the cross-indexed information is not just verbal. Television news and documentaries, as well as films, are cross-indexed and made available on videodisk, videotape, and other digital means of storage. Arthur C. Clarke proposes that his own personal television library, gathered from a dish antenna on his roof and computer indexed, is the prototype of personal libraries in the future, when each home can have the equivalent of today's library on interactive disk or tape.

In addition to commercial computer networks, the networks that interconnect universities, and through which scholars can exchange information and papers, are so vast and complex that if one seeks to diagram the flow, the world brain begins, in the eyes of some scientists, to look something like the central nervous system of humanity as envisaged by Teilhard de Chardin.[17]

The notion that this "world brain" is merely a vast computer system that synthesizes world knowledge, however, overlooks the fact that it is the human scholar, interacting with data bases, who provides the "electricity" that empowers the creative process to pursue similarities to the human brain. Professor Stephen Rosen of the City College of New York speaks also of the crucial importance of a "world heart" (we will later discuss a network of computers for compassion) if the "world brain" is not to be demonic.

Will this "world brain" be used and controlled only for the rich and privileged of the world, or will it serve universal human need?[18]

Computers Going into Education

Seymour Papert (*Mind Storms*[19]) and others have shown the potential of computers to create much better education and schools. Ted Nelson, however, warns against "computer assisted instruction" in which the workbook, which now bores pupils, is simply put on a computer screen. Alan Kay satirizes the way schools are using computers by asking if pupils would become "piano literate" if every classroom had a player piano, but no teacher knew much about music.

It is inevitable that computers are going into education to empower human minds and work. Yet there is the great danger that they will go the wrong direction, to quote Nelson, as all students are force-marched across a flattened plane, material dumped on them, "their responses calibrated, and their involvement with the material . . . not encouraged nor taken into consideration."

As computers in the workplace are being used to regiment employees and spy on them, so computers can be used to oppress students. They could also be used to inspire and empower authentic learning and growth. Who will decide where they are to go and how?

Computers Going to Politics and to War

Where are computers going? They are going not only to empower war machines, but also into politics with a vengeance (for example to provide hypertext data bases on each member of Congress to empower lobbyists).

Research firms can be hired by a political candidate to use computers to win elections: by simulating the outcome of elections on the basis of polls, by organizing political campaigns with information on every voter in a district, for desktop publishing to prepare a different personal fund-raising letter to deal with the interests or prejudices of each different voter (thus raising tens of millions of dollars as some television evangelists do).

Roger Bullis in *Computer Shock: Living and Working in a High-Tech World* tells how computers are changing the nature of government and the political process. On the positive side, he suggests that computers have the potential to create what he calls "a true democracy" by enabling better informed dialog between people and their representatives in congress. In fact, however, computers are now more likely to make it possible for politicians to manipulate and abuse the process. A computer profile is built, for example, of a congressional district, noting changes in voting patterns precinct by precinct. The profile can include information on all influential persons in each district, especially the names and addresses of persons most likely to agree with the candidate and to support her/him. Computers can then send tailored letters to everyone on specialized mailing lists of those persons.[20]

This makes it possible for a politician to capitalize on prejudices and "special interest groups" so that the candidates with sufficient funds can manipulate and abuse the electoral process. They can fight a kind of "dirty war" with the political opposition.

These same instruments can, of course, be used for compassionate and responsible political purposes if a dedicated cadre of computer programmers will develop the software.

This chapter, obviously, cannot discuss everywhere computers are going, for they are going everywhere! They are, as Stewart Brand suggests,[21] already transforming society. But who is deciding how society is to be transformed, for good or evil?

Computers that are used for sophisticated "war games" and "business gaming" are also used to design and operate vastly complex global banking systems, and can be used for exploitation. Critics say that many computer systems are too complex to be dependable. It seems inevitable that computers will continue to go to war and will be used for exploitation, as long as war and human greed continue.

It might be a gain for humans if computers and robots fought wars in such a way that human beings are not injured. But we must ask if computers can be trusted not to trigger an accidental war or global economic disaster, when systems get so complex that human beings must depend upon computers to monitor them and make lightning-swift decisions.

Will society rush ahead without adequate reflection, without giving voice to the "prophets," some of whom are listed in the footnotes of this chapter, and others who suggest better alternatives and compassionate uses for computers and who are given a hearing in the next chapter?

PROPHETS

The world of computers is inhabited by people, and each chapter introduces some of them as another way to explore this milieu, its origins and meaning. We begin with the short-short-short story of a philosopher of science, *Michael Polanyi*. He qualified in medicine in Budapest and was a medical officer during World War I. Later he became a research scientist and professor of physical chemistry. Gradually, becoming a philosopher of science, he realized that the idea of scientific objectivity is an illusion. He wrote the influential book, *Personal Knowledge* (Routledge & Kegan Paul, 1958), showing the need for scientists to admit their intellectual passions and the aesthetic content of their theory building. He set philosophy of science in the context of the worship of God.

Who will be the Michael Polanyi of the world of computers?

Ted Nelson is one of the authentic prophets or "shamans" of the world of computers. He is especially critical of those who do sloppy, half-creative work. "Any nitwit can understand computers," he says, and unfortunately, many do! "Stereotyped notions develop about computers operating in fixed ways – and so the confusion increases." He describes his book, *Computer Lib/Computer Dreams*, as a measure of desperation, written because most of what is written about computers for laypeople is either unreadable or silly.

Nelson wants to "explain the big picture," beginning with the understanding that computers are simply a necessary and enjoyable part of life, like food and books. They are not everything, he says, but they are an aspect of everything; increasingly they are in everything we use in everyday life.

He sees many in the world of computers as tending to hoard their knowledge, because knowledge is power. So, he says, "the use of computers is dominated by a priesthood, people who spatter you with unintelligible answers and seem unwilling to give you straight ones." Doctors and lawyers, he reminds us, often act the same way. Computers are too important, he says, to allow any group to have such a stranglehold on them, to let any "clique of insiders" control such important aspects of society.

The world of computers, he says, is full of "fine, imaginative people," and some brilliant ones who deserve to be better known, as computers themselves need to be better known and used by all who like mental creation, who enjoy imaginative toys, who want great new art, who want democracy and the economy to function better and with more justice.

For there is no question, he says, of "*whether* the computer will remake society. It already has. And society faces a tremendous range of options for using them in the future."

So Nelson sees it as his calling to warn against the variety of nuisances computer people have put in our lives. More important, as a prophet, he boldly stands forth to warn all of us that "the time has come to be openly attentive and critical in observing and dealing with computer systems." We should expose systems that are bad, annoying, or demeaning, just as we ought to expose pollution of the air. We should also not enlarge the "backlash," the public's mystification and irritation with computers. The public needs help to know of good and beautiful things that computers can make possible. Computers, he says, can be simple and marvelous for individuals to use, and computers belong to all people.

Nelson describes himself as a seventh-grade dropout, which may help explain his mood as he puts on his prophet's hat to declare:

> Welcome to the computer world, the damndest and craziest thing that has ever happened! But we, the computer people, are not crazy. It is you others who are crazy to let us have all this fun and power to ourselves.

Nelson says that he has little interest in improving the educational system as it is. He wants to set children on fire with enthusiasm with computer instruments that will "not be technically determined, but rather will be new realms for human artistry." Instead of hacking information up and compressing it into blocks, instead of flattening it out in linear form, we can let it blossom in all directions, we can "stretch the computer." He wants to put Renaissance humanism in a multidimensional responsive console, through his "hypertext" and "Xanadu" projects.

He began designing interactive software for personal computers in 1960, inventing one of the most creative word processing systems. He coined the terms "hypertext" and "hypermedia" (to be explained later), and wrote what may have been the world's first rock musical.

He sees himself as one of a new generation of "lunatic dreamers" who are creating transformational media. He worries that bad technology may come to dominate, crippling human thinking, yet he sees "the very real hope" for a "unified canopy of vivid and accessible information, an environment which will enhance and nurture our minds and their capabilities," taking us far beyond former levels of literacy to new levels of understanding and intelligence.

Nelson's story is perhaps still just beginning . . .

EXERCISES AND PROJECTS

1. *Bible Study*

Read Genesis 1.

Is God involved in the creation of computers? Do you see computers as compatible with the direction of God's original creation?

Read Isaiah 61, on values revealed in the Bible.

Are computers going in the direction of these values? If not, whose responsibility is it to change the direction? How could such change occur?

2. *Theological Reflection*

The following statement is for discussion by groups – teenagers, pastors, congregational study groups, bishops, mission boards, computer scientists – or for meditation by individuals.

God, the Eternal and Absolute Spirit, Crown and Source of all beauty, truth, grace, and love is – through computers – presenting us with power and knowledge by which we can become co-redeemers of creation. But if this is to happen, we must begin to develop the habits of bringing the phenomena of computer science to God for criticism and purification. With ever-increasing resourcefulness, tenacity, and creativity, the world church must now seek:

– systematic meditation on the past, present, and future of computer science;
– faithful intercession for the members of the world of computers;
– worship services geared to new responsibility and holiness in the advancement and redirection of computer technology;
– the formation of professional Christian associations of computer users;

– the search for the vision which will provide a morally, more
  morally-advanced scientific successor to all computer science;
– the construction of a tireless mission to the ideas and realities of
  computer sciences.

In that search, the whole human family will *more intimately* meet God the
Father, Son, and Holy Spirit. In this way Christ will be leading us into a
new synthesis of science and religion, a new covenant for the third
millennium, the deployment of science and religion together in behalf of
the needy. To that festival of worship, all religions can come, a hope
expressed in the theme for the First World Conference of Religious
Futurists in 1989.

3. *Theological Reading*

What are the responsibilities of the people of God in relation to the
sciences? Who are the "people of God?" See Hendrikus Berkhof, "The
People of God are the First Fruits," in *Christian Faith*, 2nd ed.
(Eerdmans, 1986), 397–414. What does it mean to identify computer
users as "people of God?"

4. *Exercises and Discussion*

We invite our readers to think about each of the directions of
computer science that we have identified in this chapter.

(*a*) Look over each "direction" (to the stars, etc.) and discuss: Is this a
possible (P1), probable (P2), or preferable (P3) future for computer
science? To find out if a "future" is preferable, ask yourself if it is
consistent with your deepest moral ideals and values.

(*b*) What would you propose as a *more preferable* future for computer
science?

(*c*) Church leaders: Ask a few members of your congregation (for
example, teenagers) to read computer journals for a month, cutting out
sections on the future of computers. Ask them to discuss with you which
of the items they would wish to consecrate to God in the offertory, and
which they would not in conscience be able to consecrate.

(*d*) Ask younger members to write to some leaders of, for example,
supercomputer research, A.I., robotics, etc., quite simply to ask:
"Where are you headed with computer research?" This might open the
door to a discussion with those leaders regarding the religious
dimension of their work.

(*e*) Where do you (individuals, church groups, computer users, etc.) think computers are going? Why?

(*f*) How did it get to be like this? What do you know about the history of computer science that shows how we arrived at these ideas?

(*g*) For organizations: Are we playing our part in finding out where computers are going, or should be going to the greater glory of God? Do we attend the meetings of the ethics division of computer science professionals organizations?

5. *Prayers*

God our Creator, Redeemer, and Sanctifier, thank you for the gift of intelligence, for your ability to love, for a share of your creativity, for our image of you within us, leading us into all truth and love. Help us now so to pray for computer research and its technological consequences, that we ourselves present your Good News to its leaders, and that by your grace the course of computer science is rapidly changed into channels of compassion and justice, that your holy will and purpose for all sciences and technologies be revealed to us, and that your Spirit sustain us as we engage in mission to, with, and by the world of computers.

6. *Meditations*

Clergy: Encourage your younger members to develop their own book of "Prayers for Computers." Sections on the following topics might make up the "chapters": the philosophy of computer science; computer scientists; computer science associations; computer users groups; computer research labs; churches as users of computers, etc.

The same book can contain meditations at the end of each section, such as this example for consideration, prayer, and reflection:

The glory of God is present in the trajectory of the history of computer science if I (we) can discern it by patient study, by contemplation, and by the loving appreciation of the efforts of computer scientists and their fellow workers in math, electrical engineering, etc. As I (we) ponder the wonders of this domain of science, God will open my(our) eyes to the still more wonderful future of compassionately-governed computers of the future, in which every step from imagination to deployment will be closely accompanied by Christ.

7. *Worship Suggestions*

Call to worship, calling attention to a computer at the center of the chancel, with arrows pointing to left and right.

Bible study: See Questions above on Genesis 1.

Presentation of news of recent developments in computer science.

Raising of specific ethical issues in computer science.

Psalm 78, and recollection of God's actions in history.

Sermon, perhaps response to this chapter.

Offertory of self and ideas (see youth project suggested above).

Holy Communion to consecrate lives dedicated to mission *to* computers.

8. *Suggestions for Further Reading*

Robert Jastrow, *The Enchanted Loom* (New York: Simon and Schuster, 1984), presents the idea of evolution passing from human being to computer. A well-written book by a leading astronomer.

Theodor Nelson, *Computer Lib/Dream Machines* (Redmond, Wash: Microsoft Press, 1987). Distributed by Harper and Row.

Stewart Brand, *The Media Lab: Inventing the Future at M.I.T.* (New York: Viking Press, 1987).

Parker Rossman, *Computers: Bridges to the Future.* (Valley Forge, Pa.: Judson Press, 1985). The effect of tomorrow's computer tools on religious thought and institutions.

Hans Moravec, *Mind Children: The Future of Robot and Human Intelligence* (Cambridge, Mass.: Harvard University Press, 1988), tells how robots will develop greater intelligence than human beings and will then replace us, another stage in evolution.

NOTES

1. See the article on varieties of Futurists in the first issue of *Futures Research Quarterly* (1985), published by the World Future Society.

2. Microsoft Press, 1987.

3. Adrian Berry, "The End of the World may Never be Nigh," *The Daily Telegraph*, London, September 3, 1986, p. 15.

4. John Barrow and Frank Tipler, *The Anthropic Cosmological Principle* (Oxford: Clarendon Press, 1985).

5. Berry, "The End of the World . . ."

6. See Hans Moravec, *Mind Children* (Cambridge, Mass.: Harvard University Press, 1988) for a current discussion of this.

7. "Exploring the Computer-Psychology Interface," *Social Science Computer Review* (summer 1988), 242, on the need for a "psychology of computers."

8. See C. J. Jung, *The Undiscovered Self* (London: Routledge & Kegan Paul, 1958), 104, *passim*.

9. "The Next Generation of Computers," *Uplink* (February 1988).

10. "Artificial Intelligence," *The Bulletin of the American Society for Information Science* (Aug.–Sept. 1988), 12: "The object of research in AI is to discover how to program a computer to perform the functions that make up human intelligence," to "create more powerful tools for man to use."

11. See Moravec, *Mind Children*.

12. See "What Philosophers say Intelligent Machines Cannot Do," American Association for Information Science Conference, (Oct. 23–27, 1988).

13. See Isaac Asimov's short story collections: *I, Robot* and *The Rest of the Robots*.

14. Cherniak, E. and McDermott, D., *Introduction to Artificial Intelligence* (Reading, Mass.: Addison Wesley, 1985), 7.

15. See Gilbert Ryle, *The Concept of Mind* (London: Hutchinson, 1949).

16. Theodore Roszak, *The Cult of Information: The Folklore of Computers and the True Art of Thinking* (New York: Pantheon Books, 1986).

17. See Pierre Teilhard de Chardin, *The Future of Man* (London: Collins and New York: Harper Colophon, 1959), 137.

18. See the cautions of H. L. and S. E. Dreyfus, *Mind Over Machine: The Power of Human Intuition in the Era of the Computer* (New York: Free Press, 1986).

19. S. Papert, *Mind Storms* (New York: Basic Books, 1980).

20. "Computer Chronicles" (May 7, 1988) reported and demonstrated many such kinds of software; for example, *Campaign Manager*, which in twenty-four hours can send out 50,000 letters to especially targeted voters.

21. S. Brand, *The Media Lab: Inventing the Future at M.I.T.* (New York: Viking, 1987).

2

It Doesn't Have To Be
The Way It Is

The world of computers has been rushing ahead with rocket speed without any significant response from prophets, from the religious communities, or from prophetic futurists. So the time has come to ask some important questions.

The present trajectory of computer science and technology is not "inevitable;" it is not pure science; it is simply a system of ideas and a subculture that enshrines certain commercial and epistemological "values."

It doesn't have to be the way it is! Computers can go in different directions!

Perhaps the time has come for "prophets" to declare a crisis and to call for an intervention into the "world of computers," to speak for a moral imperative of diverting energy, money, and inspiration into a trajectory of social compassion.

What does this mean? In the summer of 1987, a Texas child named Jessica captured the attention of much of the world when she fell deep into the narrow shaft of an unused well. Budgets and quotas were forgotten as the resources of commerce and community collaborated in a brief and frantic holy alliance to rescue her. One suffering child captured the minds of a nation. The even course of society was disrupted as the uttermost limits of engineering and imagination combined in a race against time – the race to rescue Jessica from the well.

She lives because the "Leviathan" – the great, lethargic being of society – momentarily awoke from its inertia and discovered that one of its children was perishing. Yet around the world in the greater society of "planet earth" hundreds of thousands, even millions, of earth's children were perishing as if in such a well. Helpless children are desperately ill, hungry, and do not have clean water to drink; they suffer torture and parental neglect and even slavery in some countries. Possibly as many as *one hundred thousand* such "trapped little children" die *every day* around the globe.

Once we could say that human society slept during such holocausts because people did not know. But now – in the age of computerized global communications and mass media – all influential people do know!

Across many centuries society allowed itself to ignore such crises because it seemed that little could be done for the world's ill, starving, and suffering children. Now that is no longer true in this "world of computers."

Remarkable new communication tools and other computer-operated, global-scale tools are emerging. These can inspire and empower more effective action by ordinary citizens. For example, a new type of computer software – "groupware" – brings "fusion" and "new energy" into computer conferencing by making it easy for people on several continents to collaborate and confer as if in the same room.

What we have had, when we connect people in many countries to do joint work via computer conferencing, is "fission" – something that generates power but with a lot of noise and unpleasant by-products, according to Suzanna Opper.[1] Now, however, that can change. "Groupware" begins to create fusion instead of fission. It can increase work and communication via computer networking and base it upon much better planning and much more comprehensive information. This software can help organize, rearrange, and manage long, rambling, complicated conversations and writing, cleaning up the clutter.

While the "groupware" needed to implement more effective action for compassionate purposes is still not completed, significant experiments are bringing together various kinds of technology to promote teamwork, responsibility, "synergy," and more effective demo-cracy.

Computers and Crisis Intervention

Psychologists and managers have created differentiated models of "problem solving." Part of the skill of problem solving is problem definition. Another part is deciding who "owns" the problem (jargon for who should assume the responsibility of solving it). A third part is understanding the varieties of problem-solving strategies which are available.

These vary from problem redefinition to brainstorming, from meditation to scientific reflection, from algorithmic analysis of the situation's "parameters" to crisis intervention, and some not-too-standard procedures as well. On crisis intervention, for example, the Foundation for Global Broadcasting[2] has demonstrated its LIFENET simulation of volcanic disaster warning and evacuation, connecting worldwide relief administrations with disaster experts to assist the victims of natural disasters. In fact, a part of really imaginative crisis intervention (as seen in the case of the little girl in the well) is to "break the rules" – rules of thought, conduct, "budget," and rules of "science" or creativity.

Such "breaking the rules" can make possible new and more imaginative combinations and uses of technology. Computerized television systems, for example, shift from a mode of entertainment or news to one of mobilizing every possible resource to rescue a little girl from a well – in combination with computer networks, engineering data bases, telephone and radio, medical helicopters and technology, and much more. Yet we have hardly begun to explore and demonstrate such compassionate uses of computers which can *empower* by connecting all kinds of technology to create "global-scale tools."

Under the providence of God and in the biblical view of history, it is the "people of God" (theologically "Israel" or "the church") to whom the responsibility falls for all the trapped children in "crisis wells" now and in the future.

Therefore the "people of God" (and many religious futurists contend that this includes Christians, Jews, Muslims and many other committed people of conscience as well) have, by their membership in a religious community and submission to God's will, the responsibility, under God, to "declare a crisis," to demand compassionate management of such problems as world hunger, controllable disease, and unnecessary suffering. Specifically, the *prophetic* (not the administrative) leaders of the biblical "Israel" and of the "people of God" today are the ones who can and must declare a crisis and name the nature of the crisis and possibilities for solving it.

This is happening, for example, with authors such as Earl Brewer, Jonathan Schell, Helen Caldicott, and in publications such as those of the prophetic Sojourners community in Washington, D.C., and its Sojourners magazine.

The prophet, however, has a special kind of "crisis intervention" model. The Old Testament prophet pointed to the disasters ahead if drastic action was not taken, as prophets in the area of air pollution (and the ozone layer) are doing today. The Old Testament prophets also, in the name of the Creator and Sustainer of the universe, announced a *new era, a new community, characterized by a new covenant and new relationships between God and people, and among and between the earth's people*, in which much disaster could be avoided.

The eminent Jewish historian, Robert Aron, analyzes the cultural circumstances of the childhood of Jesus in his book *Jesus of Nazareth: The Hidden Years*. He sees the birth of Judaism four thousand years ago and the birth of Christianity two thousand years ago as acts of God in the face of potential disaster. New relationships, new committed communities of people were needed. Now the twentieth century is a time of holocaust: a time of political ideologies hostile to compassion, God, and religion. In a time of Hiroshima and Nagasaki, when science and technology is often being used to kill children rather than to heal them, this Jewish scholar asks what a new divine response to the world of science should be.

Aron speculates on a new action of God today, just as the mind of Jesus came to have a higher synthesis of Judaism and the Graeco–Roman civilization of ancient Judaea. Religious prophets are announcing that such a new act of God is taking place; a new era is here. It is the era of science in which it is governed by love *at every level* of metaphysics, idea, theory, and technology. The emerging new era, sparked by the crisis in human affairs and ecology, implies a whole new kind of community, expressed globally and manifested locally as communities of scientific compassion begin to emerge in nation after nation.

This prophet calls for, and sees, the coming of an era in which art, science, and worship are unified in the ongoing, ceaseless, urgent search for those insights and life styles which will save this world's "trapped" children. This new era follows the "received" values of compassion inherited from Judaism, Christianity, and Islam. It also now aspires to give them more effective life, that is, *really* to end the hunger and suffering of so many of the world's children and indeed the anguish of their parents.

We ask if collectively, and *in toto*, this worldwide movement comprises the much-needed "world heart" – alongside the talk in the "world of computers" about an electronically-aided "world brain" – and if it is in the growth of this "world heart" that the beginnings of a new computer science can be seen. It should involve a philosophy of mathematics and technology that is governed by love of neighbor, and wherein all suffering creatures are seen as "neighbor."[3]

To sum up: computer technology can help shift the directions of teamwork and group support, and can provide clear and comprehensive information. But what about the lack of motivation?

Computers – It Doesn't Have to Be This Way

Today's science and computerized technology place tremendous power in human hands – as seen in outer-space exploration, in nuclear and "star wars" military technology, in medicine's C.A.T. (Computerized Axial Tomography) Scanners, and in brain-empowerment computer research tools. Yet where is the compassionate use of such technology for the suffering children of the Third World?

Mythically put, the message of religious futurists is this: The Lord's patience with science and technology is exhausted because God is the Lord of love. Therefore, God is now pronouncing judgment on the "world of computers" after its first hundred years or so.

God calls all responsible women and men in this milieu back to receive a new word, for the generation of a new philosophy of computer science, a new philosophy even of arithmetic or number and measurement – one which at the very least counts every hungry child in the world.

God calls for a new science, a science of mercy, and a new worldwide community of computer scientists who put social responsibility first.

Younger members of the organization "Computer Scientists for Social Responsiblity" say that it usually fails to enlist the senior scientists because they are "too busy." Too busy, we ask, where the big money is, as in star wars and nuclear destruction? Too busy to use their creativity to save the earth's air, seas, and soil from fatally poisonous pollution?

Paul Tillich spoke of three kinds of creativity proper to God: *originating* (creative acts), *sustaining*, and *consummating* (including the judgment of any artist or scientist on the success of his/her work). But God's is the power to shatter all forms, and to make over at any moment all that has gone before. This is because God is the rule-breaker as well as the law-giver. When science fails the needy, becomes selfish and fails on compassion, that science must be "shattered" and remade. God's creativity is limitless. It is directed toward all of God's children, especially the sick and the needy, and it encompasses every known kind of creativity – and more.

So today's prophets call for a new science, even an as yet unimaginably new kind; and it is through human minds that this stunning burst of creativity is coming – already now and in the future. Creativity, received in partnership with God, is mysterious, vast, awesome, and of incomprehensible magnitude.[4]

Some people do not see the stunning burst of creativity on the horizon because they think of computers only in terms of word processing, math, and science.

Motivation via Art

"The Creation Station," developed at the University of Michigan, enables teamwork by many kinds of artists – and among artists on different continents – to enhance the collaborative process.[5] It brings together computers that create music, film, videodisk, with those that enhance creativity in dance, theater, animation, and much more. Initially these computer instruments were designed for professionals, for example, for musicians on three keyboards to create music that equals two hundred symphony orchestras. However, a child can operate them and often is less inhibited than many professional adults in exploring the range of possibilities. So next – and the word suggests the astonishing "NeXT" computer, introduced by Steve Jobs in 1988 – the creation station, as it unfolds in the next few years, will provide all kinds of individuals with the means to realize their creative potential.

It works with "an intuitive interface." You and I do not yet have access to such powerful and expensive computer instruments, although one developer predicts that many such instruments will be inexpensive enough to be in primary schools within a few years. Then, however, we can use art and graphics to present needs and problems in more emotionally motivational ways. We can, for example, use the graphics potential of the MacIntosh computer plus videodisk.[6]

The *Grady Report*[7] uses the word "spectacular" for the music and art potential of the NeXT computer, which can also bring together the power to explore great literature and "social documents" interactively, with visual models "to illuminate dynamic processes." Furthermore, this new technology "is an open invitation" to all of us to greater creativity; inviting educators, for example, "to take themselves more seriously as co-creators."

One's imagination is stimulated by just glancing through the *Bookshelf Catalog* of high tech tools for music/video/film industries. Music, which by itself is tremendously important for religious and motivation groups, is accessible and creative in entirely new ways as a result of the computerized MIDI system, composing software, interactive instruments, computer-music-video systems. Inexpensive programs like "Macmovies" make it possible for the amateur to create motivation films that are much more effective than words alone.

As the night sky of radio astronomers (metaphorically speaking) is suddenly illuminated by inexplicable, gigantic energy outbursts of quasars, so God's creativity is now flaring up with enormous energy in the human community. The whole planetwide network of morally luminous minds is creating a network of ethical luminosity – the "world heart" – which, considered as the "radio telescope of the people of God," can stand alert before the limitless possiblities of God the starmaker.

Who can doubt that tremendous change is coming? We live in a time of almost unbelievable changes. In Arthur C. Clarke's novel, *The City and the Stars*, this scientific prophet writes of the "pure mentality" named Vanamonde that encompasses all times and mystifies the earthlings in the novel with his capacity to arrive before he left his point of origin. When God's creatures are suffering, God also assumes the mantle of "Lord of time" and comes for the sake of needy children – whether the world of computers is ready, is expecting or not. Television's science fiction "Dr Who", the "time lord," shows art wrestling with this theological insight.

This is a time for unexpected possibilities for the deployment of human intelligence, love, and science. The emergence of the computer industry – indeed the military-industrial complex which dominates and funds so much of this industry – is simply the product of free human choices. Choices with a different ethical basis can give us an entirely different science-technology, and an entirely different society.

What is the evidence for this assertion? We suspect that no one is ready to give a thorough philosophical answer to that question; but we invite you to read science fiction that portrays entirely different technological "rocket tracks" for human scientific and social history. In Arthur C. Clarke's short story, "The Nine Billion Names of God," for example, computers find their final fulfillment in a monastery, as suggested by the title.

Futurists also help us to see that the human story is entirely open-ended. At any time, when human society changes its mind, it can also change its science and the resulting technology.

Many religions likewise show us the possibility of free choice coupled with repentance. The message of Christianity, for example, is that it is never too late to change directions, to turn back to God in any field of enquiry, and in so doing to make a new start. Moreover, such a new beginning, the prophets assert, leads to a higher relationship to God in the spiral-shaped spiritual evolution of humankind.

In the Judeo–Christian tradition, we recall that Jesus came into Galilee saying: "Repent and believe the good news: for the kingdom of God is at hand." That word "repent" is the translation of a Greek word which means "change of heart," "change of mind," and "change of direction." Together, those three changes are a rightabout turn of direction by which persons and society reorient themselves toward God, toward goodness and compassion, toward the source of all true power.

We also recall the prophet Ezekiel, who, sitting forlornly in exile, realized that God is training people by this period of suffering; then God begins to tell the exiles that they will go home in the not too distant future. There they will build a more glorious temple than they had ever known before. Ezekiel was one of many prophets who thus called on the people to make a new beginning, and in that new beginning to find themselves on higher ground than they had ever been before.

Where are the prophets of God's people who today will announce a new beginning and a new moral direction in God's name, so that people will give a new and divine start to science itself as we enter the cosmic career of the human species, and so that planet earth is not a ghetto or the victim of unethical super-technology?

One possibility, a scenario to be expanded in chapter 4, involves possible follow-up to the first World Conference of Religious Futurists, in connection with the assembly of the World Future Society in Washington, D.C., in July 1989. Those planning that conference sought to invite philosophers of computer science to contemplate the horrors of human poverty and degradation on our planet in the context of calling for a new and higher moral direction for the computer industry. Because it "doesn't have to be this way," a consortium of theologians, futurists, science fiction writers, and computer experts, under the guidance of the Holy Spirit, were working on a systematic manifesto for the regeneration of computer science and technology.

They asserted that God has the power and that God promises to make all things new. Because the contemplation of the ethical basis of the computer milieu reveals its estrangement from religious values, a new beginning must be made. The "prophets" are announcing it, the people of God are invited to join a "festival of moral creativity" by which, in an explosion of spiritual energies, a renewed industry can be born: computers in the service of suffering humanity.

But those who make such declarations must be specific in their illustrations and examples of what this might mean, because, you ask, aren't computers already being used for significant research and education projects and other areas that are a more positive service of humanity?

Yes, but only with limited funding and insufficient imagination! Perhaps the most important judgment which the prophet must declare is really to those "half outside" the world of computers; that is to educators, religionists, social activists, and others *who merely seek to adapt for their purposes the computer technology developed for business or other commercial uses instead of entering creatively into the "world of computers" as partners, to develop computer software and technology especially dedicated to and created for the "more positive service of humanity."*

Certainly many in the "world of computers" have been giving increasing attention to "programming" for education, religion, and social service,[8] but nowhere with the sort of vision and scope seen in space and military uses of computers. Piddling little adaptations and improvisations with computer software in education and for religious institutions, for example, are hardly worthy of God in a time when millions of the world's children are ill and hungry – *and it doesn't have to be that way*!

Alternatives

In the next two chapters we will ask where computers *should* be going, and we will suggest some new directions.

Patricia Mische, co-founder of Global Education Associates, has been lecturing all over the world, pointing out that humanity now stands at a critical moment in history when we are about to make decisions – or to fail to make them – which will affect everything which follows for thousands of years. She worries that we will make these decisions – about our space exploration plans, for example – while "intoxicated with illusions" and on the basis of "historically fleeting superpower conflicts" rather than in taking adequate account of the long-range needs and direction of humanity and the perils facing our earth itself.

Those of us who ought to share responsibly in this decision-making do not adequately comprehend "the universe as a living, organic, systematic, dynamic, intelligent, divine process," she says, "of which we are all a part." She adds, "Our planet might never recover from a failure now to make the right decisions, wrong decisions made on the basis of a mechanistic, atomistic vision of the earth, in contrast to a compassionate vision of the earth, and of humanity's future, rooted in attunement to the creative process of the earth/universe."[9]

The failure of our technological era, she says, lies in the denial of "human interconnectedness to the earth and cosmic processes" and to "the denial of human interdependence within the total living earth community."

A failure of vision, she says, has brought on the breakdown of the technological age. Yet, paradoxically, computer science has enabled human beings to rediscover interconnectedness, the emergence of a global village, and the movement toward a planetary civilization.

The world of computers, and indeed of all science and technology, needs a new vision. A change of heart is coming, we suggest, from the source of all great visions, and its coming and empowerment may be enabled by the very technology that needs the vision. We will discuss this in chapter 4.

PROPHETS

Charles Babbage (1791–1871) was the first person to put forward detailed proposals for what later became the computer. From 1828 to 1839 he held the post of Lucasian Professor of Mathematics at Cambridge, though he never delivered a lecture to the university. He was a thinker and inventor. He was also a reformer. He attempted to reform the Royal Society Observatory in Greenwich. He endeavored to restructure the teaching of mathematics at Cambridge. He analyzed the operation and economics of the Post Office, the pin-making industry, and the printing trade. He published one of the first actuarial "life-tables." He made some of the earliest dynamometer measurements on the railways, running a special train on Sundays for this purpose.

In 1812 Babbage conceived a new idea, deciding that he should construct what he called a differential engine. This was a mechanical device for computing and printing tables of mathematical functions. This "engine" consisted of a set of registers, linked together by a mechanism whereby additions from one register to the next could be performed according to a fixed cycle. Babbage actually constructed a small machine with three registers. It was supposed to be able to tabulate quadratic functions to eight decimal places. After he demonstrated it in 1822, he won the support of the scientists in the Royal Society. He also received recognition from the state, the British government sponsoring his research and inventing to the tune of £17,000 – perhaps a million dollars in today's money. The machine they hoped to see never appeared during his twenty years of work, but the fruit of his work surrounds us today.

Ivan Sutherland, Ted Nelson says in *Computer Lib/Dream Machines*, is one of the "titans." He "programmed and systematized a computer setup for helping people think and work with deeply-structured pictorial information." Seldom "has an event in a new field had such power and influence as what he did between 1960–64." His thesis as a student at M.I.T. was the *sketchpad*, which could be used to draw on a computer screen instead of on paper. As a result, the computer became a powerful instrument for design.

The *sketchpad* system, Nelson says, was "at once inventive, profound, overwhelmingly impressive . . . and deeply elegant." For Sutherland "was one of the first people to understand the use of the computer in helping visualize things that weren't fully clear yet – the opposite, of course, of the conventional notion of computers. While computers had been made to do animations as early as the 1940s, and computer graphics had been put to workday duties in the old SAGE system (defending us against bombers in the 1950s . . .), Sutherland turned computer display from an inexpensive curiosity into *a true dream machine*."

The "mind-blowing thing about *sketchpad*," Nelson says, was the way you could move and manipulate the picture all over the screen, a hundred varieties in a hundred places. Sutherland brought excellence into design, enhancing creativity, showing what others seem to have missed, "what elements depended on what other elements, in a highly abstracted diagram." This, Nelson says, has remarkable possibilities.

Ivan Sutherland left the government computer program in the late 1960s to teach computer science at the University of Utah; later he founded his own company to make computer display systems. His work, Nelson claims, "has elegance and inventiveness."

Doug Englebart is responsible for word processing, and is the father of computer networking, electronic mail, outline processing, the mouse (handheld to move on a pad to operate a computer), dividing the screen into windows, and the work station which makes it possible for people to work together on a larger and more significant scale.

Nelson says that although Englebart is well known in the world of computers, he should be better known and appreciated by the public. In fact, "his chosen mission should be known to all."

He began his work as an engineer working on cathode-ray tubes, which Nelson calls "lightning in a bottle." At the Stanford Research Institute in California, millions of dollars were spent on his dream (Nelson calls it a wonder and a glory) of expanding human minds and "improving each shining hour." Englebart's vision, Nelson says, has never been restricted to the technical – merely to put people in front of display consoles to labor – but has been to make minds work better "by giving them better tools to work with."

Englebart saw that people could write better and think better with computer instruments that could double and redouble intellectual capacities. So his work laid the foundation for word processing, the largest and most important use of computers. He has been called "a saintly man" whose dream has been to enhance people's intelligence and to bring them together more effectively and creatively.

To make his point he once tied a pencil to a brick and had someone write with it to show what can happen with tools that make such work harder and more inflexible. What can make intellectual work easier and less vague is a system (like Hypertext) in which everything you are working on is interconnected with everything else – footnotes, source materials, comments, and ideas. In this way one's mind can take flight, one's ideas can soar.

Nelson points out that in the German language, "Englebart" has the word angel in it; and Englebart "is indeed on the side of the angels." His work and inventions point a new way for humanity.

EXERCISES AND PROJECTS

1. *Bible Study*

Read Isaiah 57:11 to 58:12.

In what sense are computers, supercomputers, smart robots, etc. "gods" (57:11)? What would it mean for computer science to "return to God" (57:14)?

What may happen to those computer scientists who serve God and who work to regenerate computer science under God's power and direction (58:8–12)?

What needs to happen to the "house of computer science" (58:12)?

2. *Theological Reflection*

All power belongs to God. Nothing is beyond God's omnipotence.

Thus God has power not only to call a complete halt to that cultural phenomenon which we call science, but to redeem and regenerate it. It is the responsibility of the people of God to claim that power and to exercise it by prolonged praise, meditation, worship, and creativity, with the result of a new (more compassionate) computer science by the year 2000.

God's power can be "wielded" or exercised by scientists, engineers, entrepreneurs as well as by prophets, pastors, and theologians. Waiting on God's power and purpose can produce serendipitous results. Let us begin a worldwide time of prayer and waiting on God's transforming word for computer science.

3. *Theological Reading*

See Paul Tillich, "The Shaking of the Foundations," his sermon in the book bearing the same title (London: SCM Press, and New York: Scribner, 1948).

4. *Exercises and Discussion*

For small groups in churches, computer-user groups, science fiction clubs in schools, colleges, etc.: If you could go back in time to the beginning of computer science (for example, study Charles Babbage, 1791–1871; see his biography in this chapter) and if you wanted to give the whole phenomenon of computer science a new start in Christ, what would you do? What would be different?

Now imagine that you can make such a new start now. What is the first step in beginning an entirely new line of moral or compassionate computer science? Imagine that you have made a trip to a nearby star where an "Other Earth" has developed such a computer science. What, in this imaginary journey, is the "first generation" of computers like, and what is the sixth generation like? What are computers doing there?

For science clubs, youth groups, or schools: From where did computer science emerge? Why? Whose choices created this stream of culture? Is computer science "pure" in the eyes of the Holy Spirit? What kind of computer science would be?

For theologians: What kind of event would need to occur if there was to be (a) a regeneration of computer science in Christ, and (b) a completely new line of mathematics leading to a divine science, paralleling computer science but enshrining the values of Christ?

For "prophets" (for example, people identified as planners by their denomination): What is the Word of the Lord to computer science? To math and science teachers: How can God use you to create a new moral trajectory for computer science? What "new thing" is God doing? What should be the "response of the people of God?" How can we receive the power of God?

For persons or groups in the "world of computers:" Take a few minutes to practice "repentance," that is, to examine conscience to identify faults, sins, crimes, etc., in relation to that world. (Note the criticisms of Ted Nelson reported here earlier.) Do this on behalf of yourself, your group (company or church), on behalf of your nation, on behalf of the computer industry, and on behalf of the whole human race. Describe what you would be doing if from now on you relate to the world of computers in a way that is free from the errors or sins you have identified. Engage in some kind of action that reflects your willingness to live in this new way, be it in your religion, your study, your science, your industry, your prayer, or your relationships.

Note to theologians: This exercise integrates "ascetical theology" with science, and also possibly with commerce/industry. What remains is to substitute *the feeding of the world's hungry* for the idea of personal ecstasy as the central element in the climax of ascetical theology: mystical theology. For then "spirituality" will have been affected by the crisis spoken of in this chapter.

5. *Prayers*

Congregations might construct prayers to God the Creator, Redeemer, and Holy Spirit to help the world church to discover the scientific and philosophical roots of computer science, and to lay down new, morally-correct roots. For example:

God, Creator of all things, we now pray that you will re-create the history of computer science, planting (this time) at its core your divine mercy and justice. Help us then to retrain our young people so that they can help this more compassionate science to grow truth and to deliver a rich and glorious fruit for the suffering, needy world.

Lord Christ, Great Redeemer, thank you for your mystical body, the holy church. Thank you for dying for us and rising again in great splendor. We acknowledge our weakness and the lukewarm nature of our faith and our discipleship. Accept our prayer for the redemption and regeneration of computer science, and place your redemptive power and direction at the very center of the world of computers. This being done (we claim in faith), show us, Lord, the way forward for all your church leaders in this your world.

Blessed Holy Spirit, you are the Lord of all power. Grant to us the coming of yourself with great power and brilliancy, so that as we now set out on the journey of the regeneration of the history of computer science, and as we aim to bring the power of the Holy Spirit to the world of computers, you are ahead of us as a pillar of fire, and you come to us as the inward purifying fire. Lord, Holy Spirit, you are the radiant energy of divine love and purity. May our flame of goodness engulf us and warm us with your own joy, as we share in the victory of Jesus who has overcome the world.

6. *Meditations*

A *New York Times* review (April 24, 1988) of Gregory Benford's science fiction novel, *Great Sky River* (New York: Spectra/Bantam, 1988), tells the story of a time when terrified human beings flee from the encroachments of intelligent machines that reduce people to a machine level, while the "machine intelligences reveal themselves to be artists of a kind." The reviewer says that what is most memorable in the book is the "central image of humans on the move, reluctant nomads in a hostile environment, reliving nightmares from the ancestral past . . . struggling for the continuation of the species." The book "offers more than a whiff of religious symbolism."

In the following meditation, the "I" or "we" can be used as appropriate for an individual or group.

There is a crisis in human affairs; I am a part of it. Around the world my brothers and sisters are in a desperate way. I feel their agony. God-in-me can act with stunning power and immediacy, if only I can allow God's energies to "surface" in me and the gospel to shatter the improper forms of science and computer science, to smash the idols of our culture's prized technology. So, then, I pledge myself to stand at permanent alert (at the level of my soul) on behalf of the progressive and accelerating transformation of the sciences so that they serve the children of the world – like the one who fell into the well in Texas – with moral power and the resourcefulness of the ever-living, ever-coming God. Through me, then, innovative new science, philosophy of science, and forms of church/service are entering the world. In this way, God is coming with breathless haste to the needy of the world. The whole people of God are redeeming the world of science and technology, to this end, with ever-increasing speed and accuracy.

7. *Suggestions for Further Reading*

Histories of computer science such as: S. H. Hollingdale and G. C. Toothill, *Electronic Computers* (Harmondsworth: Penguin Books, 1965); E. A. Feigenbaum and Pamela McCorduck, *The Fifth Generation: Artificial Intelligence and Japan's Computer Challenge to the World* (London and Sydney: Pan Books, 1983).

On mathematical philosophy: Bertrand Russell, *Introduction to Mathematical Philosophy* (London: Allen and Unwin, 1980); Morris Kline, *Mathematics: The Decline of Certainty* (New York: Oxford University Press, 1980).

On the identification and nurture of brilliance in education: L. M. Terman, ed., *Genetic Studies of Genius*, 4 vols. (Palo Alto: Stanford University Press, 1925–1957); J. P. Guilford, "Creativity," *American Psychologist* (vol. 5, 1950), 444–54.

On using science fiction to expore possible futures see "Science Fiction as an Educational Tool" in Alvin Toffler, *Learning for Tomorrow: The Role of the Future in Education* (New York: Random House, 1974).

On divine power, Colin Urquhart, *Holy Fire* (London: Hodder and Stoughton, 1982).

NOTES

1. "In Strength in Numbers: Groupware May Revolutionize the Way We Work," *Computerworld* (August 3, 1988).

2. 3251 Prospect St. N.W., Washington D.C. 20007.

3. *Tranet*, for example, reports on "appropriate technology" organizations all over the world (Box 567, Rangeley, Maine 04970).

4. Those who wish to read more on such theological ideas are referred to Nicolai Berdyaev.

5. See David Gregory, "Fine and Performing Arts: The Creation Station," *Academic Computing* (October 1988).

See Nick Iuppa and Karl Anderson, *Interactive Video Design* (White Plains, N.Y.: Knowledge Industries Publications, 1987); *CD–ROM: The New Papyrus*, (Redmond, Wash.: Microsoft Press, 1986); Sueann Ambron and C. Hooper, *Interactive Intermedia* (Redmond, Wash.: Microsoft Press, 1988).

7. Oct. 12, 1988.

8. Significant beginnings are seen in such periodicals as *Computers and the Humanities* and the *Social Science Computer Review*.

9. "The Soul of the Universe," *Fellowship* (Oct.–Nov. 1986).

3

Where *Should* Computers Be Going?

Who is assigned to "critique" the "world of computers" as films and books are reviewed in the press? Computer software and creations are, for the most part, reviewed in newspapers and magazines only to ask (1) if they achieve their self-defined purposes, the goals of those who created them, and (2) if they are successful, that is, make money.

We have cited some authors who are questioning goals in the world of computers, but industry leaders themselves often seem to rush ahead without pausing to check moral or compassionate road maps or to debate their sense of direction.

So the prophet – whether futurist, social critic and philosopher, media reviewer, or whoever – should ask some fundamental questions about where computers should be going, what unmet needs are crucial.

What would a prophet like Joel suggest? He might be tempted to list all the world's problems, so we focus here on a few examples.

Go to the Crippled and Helpless

First, a prophet would suggest that computers should be going to shut-ins, including paralyzed and handicapped persons, to live with them, empower them, and enable them to live rich and productive lives. One hears of "killer robots" in car factories that occasionally spot weld persons instead of joints. By contrast, the time has come for "caring robots" to go to helpless people, to do their chores, provide companionship, and make it possible for them to be connected to the outside world. On an experimental basis, some totally paralyzed and helpless persons are now living happy and productive lives – even though they can't leave their rooms – studying, working, being entertained, visiting friends, etc., all via computer networks; and in a computerized room with computerized servants.

For example, health care for shut-ins is highly improved by a computer in Boston that a physician can use to monitor five hundred patients at home, alerting the physician to changes in blood pressure, to dangers that require immediate attention, etc.[1] At a psychiatric hospital related to Albert Einstein Medical School in New York City, ex-patients are provided with computers and modems to keep in close touch with the hospital, and to create support groups of patients with similar problems so they can help look after each other. This, combined with some avant-garde, computer-empowered education on what to do when leaving the institution, has been quite successful in enabling mental patients to survive on their own in difficult parts of the city so that they do not end up as homeless persons on the streets.

Asimov's laws of robotics represent "a negative ethic:" what robots should not do. Christians ought to be proposing a "positive ethic" for robots; they should help the helpless (some British children speak of "helplots" for this kind of compassionate robot). Meanwhile, emerging computer developments – which badly need support – are helping the crippled to walk, the blind to see (like Stevie Wonder's instruments), the deaf to hear. Compassionate people in the "world of computers" should seek to complete such instruments for all those in the world who need them, mass produce them to reduce costs.

When Saw We Ye Hungry?

Second, a prophet would suggest that computers should be going wherever there is hunger, suffering, degradation, illness, and hopelessness. Properly programmed, for example, powerful new computer instruments could empower those who seek to help suffering children everywhere. In the region where desert is spreading south of the Sahara, computer instruments are already used at the United Nations to understand the origins of famine and to govern the logistics of food production and distribution. With more public support, portable computers – as terminals and empowerment instruments – and their expert systems could be on their way to the trouble spots of the world whenever necessary.

This is not just a dream or theoretical "idea." What a compassion network could do is already demonstrated in the world of "Car(e)net," a computer connection among development workers in various Third World countries; and by "PeaceNet," an international computer conferencing network of peace activists all over the world. Anyone with a computer and modem can, at modest cost, connect with PeaceNet to send instant messages (E-mail) to peace activists elsewhere to get information about what is going on in peace work, to participate in ongoing peace discussions, to get access to computer bulletin boards used to coordinate specific action projects, etc. An effort is being made to coordinate all other on-line peace conferencing and computer coordination (including that of various denominations) with and through PeaceNet.

Such networking for more effective action is also empowered with computer coordinated information: computer data bases. For example, monks in Germany have for some time been working on a computer data base to catalog and coordinate all existing information on peacemaking, past and present. PeaceNet now seeks to coordinate such existing data bases as well as to help create new ones. The many data bases listed in the PeaceNet index include, *for example*:

– peace law cases database;
– Beyond War Foundation database;
– Central American Resource Netework data on human rights, alerts, congressional news, political and military events;
– Center for Innovative Democracy.

Such data bases can be cross-indexed and updated regularly to provide any needed information at once; and in time can be assessible via a special satellite for library information. Or a vast amount of data-base information can be made available much more inexpensively on CD–ROM or videotape with new processes now developed to provide such information very cheaply to libraries or to share-cost groups.

The work of caring for hungry children in various countries, on the PeaceNet model, could also be empowered by the use of computer bulletin boards to share information and coordinate activities. Any person can check bulletin boards on PeaceNet each day for the latest information. When we last looked the PeaceNet bulletin boards included, for example:

– Center for a New Democracy working paper on improving US–USSR relations;
– design discussion for a transnational network;
– reports of the Foundation for the Arts of Peace;
– news of the National Peace Institute foundation (which works with and supports the new federally funded U.S. Institute of Peace);
– Star Wars Alternative Network catalog of options.

Action to help the world's hungry or any other such project can be further facilitated by on-line computerized directories. Anyone interested in helping or just getting information can use the computer network to secure materials and addresses and phone numbers of individuals and organizations, all regularly updated. Such directories can be local, as illustrated by ecumenical computer bulletin boards in some cities which now provide pastors and congregations with help for any emergency or social service need. Until one consults a directory on PeaceNet or elsewhere, for example, one may not know of:

– the International Peace Research Association (interconnected peace research institutes in many countries);
– the UN Institute (and related international groups seeking to change the United Nations to make it more functional);
– HARBINGER, which creates data base systems to use university mainframe computers for sharing information on peace issues;
– etc.

Planning and other committee functions, to reduce meeting expense greatly, can be conducted via computer conference networks. For example, a yearlong conference was held on NWI (Networking and World Information) to plan and coordinate a November 1987 conference at United Theological Seminary in Ohio on "The Church in a Digital Age." All of the speeches or papers to be presented were put "on-line" on the computer network so that those who might attend could read them in advance and contribute to their revision before and after the conference. This made possible a unique kind of conference in that there were few actual speeches. The participants could spend their time in small-group discussion to improve and enlarge the ideas proposed by the "speakers" in advance.[2]

– On the EIES network, for example, there has been an ongoing computer conference (from London) on "participatory democracy" which involved people on three continents in ongoing discussion (the EIES network is from the New Jersey Institute of Technology);
– also on EIES: specific peace actions were coordinated on a specially set up computer peace conference (EIES, we note, has also coordinated military planning);
– a computer conference on PeaceNet has been discussing a strategy for developing mutual security as US Policy;
– a third has been discussing a global conflict management system;

– the Star Wars Alternative network has had an ongoing conference on computers and peace gaming and simulations.

Empowering Ordinary People

Third, computers should be going to where the systems are chaotic, making it simpler to get into world information banks or to use computer networks and systems. New systems and software are needed to "help make the crooked ways straight." Teams of ethically oriented computer specialists – and many individuals – can hear the prophetic call for developing alternatives to the jargon or to the confusing and conflicting procedures and systems that make it difficult for many people to enter the "world of computers." Where the complexity of information and data basis becomes so overwhelming as to be frustrating and unmanageable, "ethical" computer science can unravel the complexity by aiding in the establishment of priorities and in eliminating the unessential (for example, helping the elderly with tax returns).[3]

Perhaps nowhere can computers do more harm or be of more help to humanity than in politics. Instead of being used to mystify and manipulate voters, computers should go to legislatures and to the leaders of national and international governments, political agencies and parties, with procedures to help make politics more participative, to be a source of empowerment for each constituent and each sector of society (neighbourhood, region, or local action group).

As the world grows in population and complexity, democracy, to thrive and expand, needs computers. Roger Bullis in *Computer Shock: Living and Working in a High-Tech World* (the book is available on computer diskette as well as in printed form) tells how computers are already changing the nature of government and the political process to make it possible. The dangers Bullis sees – illustrated by the way polls can change the outcome of an election with computerized analysis of preliminary returns before many people have the chance to vote – can be overcome through methods developed by Richard Spady.

A businessman in Seattle, Washington, Spady has developed a computer system to transform the political process, in church as well as state governance, and yield the possibility of a moral breakthrough within political science itself. He found that many church people feel that decisions are made for them in which they are not adequately consulted. So Spady set up a comprehensive computerized polling process with many alternatives, rather than just two (for or against), as in most public opinion polls. Polls are combined with many small-group discussions to make sure that people understand the issues before the poll and its sophisticated analysis.

This use of computers makes it possible to gather, tally, and coordinate the information in ways that never were possible before. This has been so successful that legislation has been proposed for a statewide use of the process to involve large numbers of people in hearings and discussion in major political issues. The Roman Catholic Archdiocese of Seattle used Spady's computerized process to involve 80,000 Catholic laypeople in interactive discussion of church issues, a fundamental step in the direction of church democracy.

Such computer-operated procedures for mobilizing collective intelligence and for computer networking can make possible a potential leap forward in the entire basis of the governance of humanity and society. Entirely new dictatorship-shaking concepts of the "polis" (city-state of ancient Greek times) are coming to birth in this way and are dramatically expanding the options of citizens for thinking about and participating in their own governance and commonwealth, as seen in the changes of governance in Eastern Europe.

Brother Austin David Carroll, formerly a researcher at IBM who has set up computer services for the Catholic Archdiocese of New York, has pioneered in theory for using computer modeling and simulations in training specialists in peace making. He proposed, for example, developing computer models of the way global politicians think on issues of peace and war. His is not just a theoretical idea. One computer model of the thinking of one U.S. Secretary of State already exists.

Graduate students and faculty members in various university departments of political science have created significant models of global politics, win/win and other alternatives.[4] Have any church universities or Christians sought to be involved in this process?

Two Christian futurists have been involved in demonstrations of computer connections between universities in various countries in the hope of interconnecting departments of political science and graduate students on such topics for joint modeling and simulating of new alternatives in global politics. For example:

– for a global parliament on a computer network;
– for the world court (playing out possibilities of cases that nations at present are unwilling to take to the court via computer simulations);
– for comparing laws of all nations in order to build up a computer data base of "world law" (a compilation of laws that all nations agree

upon, which can therefore be applied to international human rights, etc.) in contrast to "international law" which deals only with relationships between nations;
– new alternatives for conflict resolution, for preventing crises and dealing with crises, including peace gaming.

Computer "peace gaming" explores alternative-to-war games, to be explored on anyone's personal computer. Some instructional computer games for university students can continue to grow into larger and more significant projects for exploring peace alternatives.[5] A significant example is the ICONS program at the University of Maryland which interconnects students via computer conferencing to play out international crises. Students at different universities in the USA or in other countries play the part of political leaders of various nations.

Some military people involved in computer war games spend some hobby time using the technology to explore alternatives to war. This led Bob Graetz of EDEN (an innovative computer conferencing group) and Bob Smith, a former space administration official, to propose enlarging the term "peace game" to "transformational-security gaming" in the hope that both doves and hawks can do some experimental cooperation. Its aim, Graetz says, should be to involve large numbers of ordinary people who are interested in transforming the war system into a peace-development system.

One advantage of computer-modeling-and-simulation is that it can provide, without risk, a way to try more controversial alternatives to war. The term "game" suggests that it is possible "in a spirit of play" for political leaders to try things out that they feel are impossible for them to try officially. Simulations might be used to play with proposals such as:

– Robert Muller's (the United Nations University of Peace) proposal to begin a continuing computer conference on global governance by one hundred of the world's best minds; or his suggestion of ongoing and regular electronic conferencing links between heads of states and the United Nations;
– Michael Shane's suggestion[6] of a global computer network of local governments to help people solve their own problems locally, and Newcomb's proposal for a similar association of small nations;
– Takeshi Utsumi's demonstrations of simulated peace games.[7]

Everyone Empowered and Responsible

Where should computers be going? Into everyone's life to empower individuals to take charge of their own lives and to help solve their own problems; in preventive medicine, for example, to reduce costs of health care and to improve the quality of health care everywhere in the world. Computers can help do this as they are used to develop working models of positive health – body, mental, and spiritual; and to keep more comprehensive holistic medical records on each person.[8] Computer hyperwebs, interrelated data from many sources, can lead us to "hyper-health" on a global basis.

In medicine and elsewhere, one way individuals are already being empowered is by the placement of more information into our hands than was ever before possible.

Computers are making possible a global electronic encylopedia/ university which already includes the theological tradition and holy scriptures – as the libraries of the world's universities go on line. But who is questioning the coding system for all the world's knowledge, which is itself the product of ethical choices and priorities? When those choices (in the Western and Christian subdivisions of the global encyclopedia) are guided by God's self-revelation and by the Holy Spirit, the categories which emerge can lead to a different concept of knowledge, a different way of organizing the information, and a different set of options for the users of the emerging global electronic encyclopedia. For example, scientific information could also be organized around central categories, such as the needs of the elderly or the whereabouts of malnourished children, rather than just around the stock exchange prices in Tokyo or the prospect of the futures market in Chicago.

The coming of the global encyclopedia, with its integration of different bodies of knowledge, can be accompanied by the long-awaited integration of the spiritual and the scientific which now interests many physicists. The gulf between these two ways of knowing has resulted in a technology divorced from God and in the consequent horrors of war and abuse of technology in the twentieth century. As this gulf is bridged, Christians can look to a twenty-first century in which computer science (and all sciences and technology) proceeds from a deep and perpetual encounter with the Spirit of God in the varieties of mental prayer, meditation, and worship experiences.

Computers Must Go to Church

Computers are now "going to church" (and synagogues, mosques), but properly? The issue for religious people is not "what computers can do" but "what God's people will do with computers." Those religious leaders who ignore computers, who do not get involved, should ask themselves if they would have done the same thing at the time the printing press was invented. Would they have not used that new technology, leaving it only for the pornographers to use?

As printing has done across several centuries, computers too can help empower the church in nearly every area of its work, including mission and pastoral care, worship, and in the analysis of religious experience.

For example, with computer-empowered education, the church, even the small parish with few children and meager resources, can again provide pioneering demonstration models of what now (with multimedia computerized textbooks and other individualized programs) ought to take place in the education of all the world's children.[9] This cannot happen if the churches merely seek to adapt inadequate commercial software now available to schools (and if educators simply seek to adapt computer instruments prepared for business, or merely seek to replicate what is already failing in existing schools).

We note that a Presbyterian computer network pioneered connections to Geneva and Africa, and to a theological school in Mexico, to enlarge its educational resources. If churches in the last generation could build a vast network of mission colleges, hospitals, and agricultural stations all over the world, then can't the next generation develop all kinds of computer software and greatly expand horizontal computer networking?

Perhaps among of the most important interpersonal things happening in our time are the horizontal relationships being developed, often greatly facilitated by teleconferencing and computer conferencing through so-called space bridges. People establish direct relationships with people in other countries without going through governments or international agencies. For example, a town in Montana develops a partnership with a comparable town in Siberia; and soon an American congregation will use computer networks to sustain "sister church" relationships with a congregation in Asia or Africa.

Other kinds of horizontal relationships are equally important. For example, many congregations have only one or two people who are interested in a particular cause (such as African famine). So the few people in a congregation who serve on such a task force often feel that no one else is interested. Such isolated individuals who are concerned about famine, and small organizations that feel weak and alone, can be empowered through computer conference relationships, on an ongoing basis, with other individuals and groups. The denominational conferences on the NWI, Networking and World Information computer network, are a notable example. These can greatly strengthen regional church committees – denominational in a region, ecumenical in a country – that are working on a particular issue.[10] Such a computer data base of church members can be used to mobilize people for all kinds of study, action, or research, whether by a congregation, a group of churches, or by a national coordinating agency.

Research? Yes, computers can empower every group for more effective learning and for new kinds of religious research and experimentation. For example, computers should be going to monasteries (old types and new) so that the significance for mission of the "varieties of religious experience" can be appraised and integrated into the prayer life of the worldwide church. Monks, old kinds and new kinds, can be accountable to one another for various kinds of experimentation: in developing community, prayer, and disciplined meditation; they can also report to one another, using a central electronic data base, on the relationships they discover between spiritual discipline and their own actual empowerment for mission. Thus experimentation with prayer, for example, can advance toward becoming a true science, worthy to become "queen of the sciences" in an authentic experimental sense.

Similarly, every local church could use computers for becoming a spiritual laboratory. Computer-organized relational data bases could make it possible for every member to practice a type of prayer and then report on its value to the community as a whole. Admittedly, this can be a painful transition from narcissistic types of praying, but it can be exciting!

What can be done with experimentation with types of individual prayer can also be done for worship and other group spiritual experimentation. Types and models of worship can be quite systematically analyzed for their *consequences* for mission, for empowering the calling of individual scientists and others. Thus worship and congregational life can intersect with experimental science. This idea should be considered in the context of the suggestion of the philosopher Albert North Whitehead, that religion as a cultural force is still in its

beginning phase.[11] Worship, like religion, is still a young under-
developed cultural force in human history, and its best days are to come.
   In *Science and the Modern World*, Whitehead wrote:

> The immediate reaction of human nature to the religious vision is
> worship. Religion has emerged into human experience mixed with
> the crudest fancies of barbaric imagination. Gradually, slowly,
> steadily the vision recurs in history under nobler form and with
> clearer expression. It is the one element in human experience whch
> persistently shows an upward trend . . . the worship of God is not a
> rule of safety – it is an adventure of the spirit, a flight after the
> unattainable. The death of religion comes with the repression of the
> high hope of adventure.[12]

Who Owns the Problem?

It is easy to say what ought to happen. This discussion of where
computers *ought* to go could be continued for chapter after chapter, but
who is responsible for nudging computer science in some new
directions? To put it bluntly, if computers are not going where ethicists
or prophets say they should be going – and this is truly a problem for the
future of society – who *owns* that problem? That is, who is going to do
something about it?
   In chapter 2 we introduced the idea of problem-solving methods to be
used by the "people of God" in relation to the world of computers. One
such method, we noted, is *crisis intervention*. It is well suited to helping
the suffering and the desperate.
   In asking where computers *should* be going, we need to introduce
another important "skill" of problem solving: identifying *who owns the
problem*. It is one thing to prescribe directions for computers and their
makers. It is another to identify the persons responsible for the
redirecting. Here theology and Bible study can introduce an important
truth. This can be formulated quite systematically as a theological axiom
on moral excellence in the world of computers.

> In the "world of computers," as society explores issues in the
> advancement of ethics and morality, when attention is turned to the
> world of religion, the practice of compassion and the extension of the
> scope of true worship and justice, it is *the people of God* who "own the
> problem" of where computers should be going.

This statement needs some explanation. It has to be thought about, entertained with a generous spirit, and interpreted in the light of the biblical understanding of human history.

First, we need to consider what it is *not* saying (all appearances to the contrary, perhaps!). Theological statements are often not quite what they seem; theology sometimes has to be the language of paradox. Theology, like all systems of knowledge and communication, that is, all sciences, uses abbreviation, "codes" (though not secret ones!) and "shorthand" phraseology (familiar only to its regular users). So when we say that "the people of God" own the problem, we are not making a "triumphalistic" statement. We are not saying that God's elect are such morally clever people that only they know what to do.

What we are saying is that those with an orientation toward the study of ethics, who seek to nurture conscience, who make a more disciplined effort to study and to understand, are responsible to society to engage faithfully in that study and to share what they learn.

Society is made up of specialist groups. One kind of work is expected from scientists: for example, the discovery of patterns and order in the natural world. Another kind of work is expected from philosophers and ethicists: for example, the application of wisdom and the enlargement of vision to see long-range implications. Society expects still another thing from its religious prophets and theologians: the identification of the will and power of God (a faithful judgment on the failure to include love and compassion as the energizing center of that science and philosophy).

A great theme of Judaism and Christianity is identification of "the people of God." This phrase does not necessarily mean the lucky ones, but those who undertake the responsibility of spiritual adventuring and moral pioneering.

In the nineteenth century there was an American "type" of frontiersman who set out for the western frontier, often in wagon trains, maybe under the slogan "Oregon or bust!" Not every American headed thus for the frontier. Some stayed in New England. Those suited by temperament, skill, and perhaps by physique became the pioneers. They headed west. In salvation history, as the Bible portrays it, there have been similar pioneering individuals and groups.

Abram left Haran to "found a nation under God;"
Moses left Egypt to lead a people chosen for a mission in history;
the apostles of Jesus established the beginnings of a loving, global community.

They were moral and spiritual frontiersmen. The communities they founded were also a stream of people – pioneers – and the sum of all such spiritual "frontiersmen" equals the "people of God."

Theologians speak of the people of God as persons "elected," a servant people. This "election" is more than election for personal salvation. A more mature attitude toward "the mystery of election" (God also gives special opportunities to talented musicians and scientists) sees it in terms of the responsiblities of service and of suffering for righteousness' sake.

It is interesting to notice how science fiction writers develop this theme in terms of genetic mutation: the people of God as moral mutants, the first of a new species. This theme is developed in Olaf Stapledon's novel *Odd John*, in A. C. Clarke's *Childhood's End*, also in John Wyndham's *The Midwich Cuckoos*. But what is important is to realize that "election" (politicians, please note!) implies vocation or calling.

Vocation can be understood in terms of human talent and psychology. Some people are metaphorically called to be symphony conductors or sports professionals. This can also be understood theologically: God calls out from society those with a "talent" or sensitivity for the things of God, for the nurture of love and compassion. This God does by the Spirit, which leads people to an awareness of their relationsip to God as "suffering servant," to an awareness of "calling" or vocation.

Society knows that there are "people of God," sociologically speaking. Even secular sociologists recognize the place in society of mystics, prophets, ecstatics, and divines. Indeed, geneticists increasingly ascribe to religion in general[13] a survival value in terms of natural selection. And just as society funds and supports science, expecting knowledge of nature in return, so it funds and supports religious communities, expecting knowledge of God and God's will in return.

This leads to a second theological axiom for those applying divinity studies to the world of computers:

> The world's religious communities must take the lead in showing and enacting "where computers *should be* going."

That statement may not be true for all time, but it is true now. And it leads to another important point about theological or prophetic statements: they are very particular!

The Word of God to the biblical prophets was very particular for a specific situation, and very personal. For example, Elijah, recovering from his depression and loneliness ("I alone am left"), received very exact instruction in his vision of the Lord's directive. He was told to visit particular persons: ". . . anoint Hazael as king of Syria . . . Jehu son of Nimshi as king of Israel . . . Elisha son of Shaphat from Abel Meholah to succeed you as prophet" (I Kings 19:10, 15–16).

Biblical directives are not vague generalities: they are specific. Therefore, when we say that the people of God "own the problem" of new moral directives to computer science, we are saying pointedly that the world's religious leaders are responsible to God and society to think, speak, lead, and act – with power, energy, resource, and speed – to propose a new, divine direction to the world of computers.

This leads us to our third theological axiom:

The world's religious leaders need to cooperate in developing a shared curriculum of divinity studies and computer studies.[14]

This book seeks to be a beginning for that task, and a stimulus for more adequate preparation.

The study of vocation is a deep and fruitful one for religious leaders who are involved in the "world of computers." Churches need to develop a theology of vocation with reference to the sciences, such that the right questions can be asked of young science enthusiasts, etc., especially those who are practicing members of religious groups. Such questions as "Do you think God is calling you to a vocation in the world of computers?" are suggested at the end of this chapter. These questions need to be asked by mission boards, ministry assessment panels, ordination examiners, seminary deans, and college admissions officers to find those who have such a calling.

When they are identified, they need to be trained, supported, cared for, equipped, and launched into their God-given work: seeking to help people with a vocation jointly to divinity studies and natural science to recognize that vocation, and to act upon it by finding membership in a community of like-minded people.

Their task, we suggest, is "computers for compassion" and perhaps some new technology as discussed in the next chapter.

PROPHETS

Dietrich Bonhoeffer (1906–1945) has become famous to many persons as a kind of ideal of the modern, "relevant," practical-minded theologian. Born in Germany, he was the son of a professor of psychiatry. He grew up in academic surroundings, and in 1930 he was appointed lecturer in systematic theology at Berlin University.

In 1933, on the wireless, he denounced Hitler and his ideas. Two years later, after a time in England, Nazi authorities banned him from Berlin and forbade him to teach. At the outbreak of World War II and against the advice of friends, he gave up the security of the U.S.A., where he was lecturing. He returned to Germany to work for the banned "Confessing Church" and the political opposition to Hitler. He was arrested in 1943 and, two years later, following imprisonment in Buchenwald, he was hanged at Flossenburg.

During the years of the Third Reich, Bonhoeffer was principal of a small experimental and technically illegal theological college on the Baltic coast of Germany. Apart from his many books on theology, such as *The Cost of Discipleship* and *Life Together*, his posthumous papers and letters from prison revealed the coming-to-birth in his mind of a "new theology" known to post-war theologians as "religionless Christianity." Along with "process theology," Bonhoeffer helps provide a sense of direction for planning mission to computers.

Consider: Where are the "Bonhoeffers" of today who will lay down their lives – or at least their ideas! – so as to equip themselves to take the gospel of love into the world of computers? What new, experimental theological communities are even now being formed in Germany or wherever to practice Bonhoeffer's "life together" in the mission to this technological world?

Takeshi Utsumi is a Christian Japanese scientist who has great dreams about where computers should go, and who has been conducting a series of global-scale demonstrations of possibilities in order to challenge the entire "world of computers" in education, science, and politics to think in much larger and more service-oriented terms.

He was educated at Tokyo Institute of Technology and then went to America as a Fullbright scholar at the University of Nebraska and Montana State University; he received his Ph.D. at the Polytechnic Institute of New York. He has diversified scientific experiences with American and Japanese firms, including the Mitsubishi Research Institute and the Mobil and Shell Oil Companies, specializing in computer simulation and optimization of petrochemical and refinery processes. He has also lectured, consulted, and pursued research in hybrid computation, process control, management science, systems science, and engineering at the University of Michigan, Louisiana State

University, the University of Pennsylvania, M.I.T., the East–West center, and several Japanese universities.

He became dissatisfied with business corporations and scientists who were interested only in profits, and who showed little concern for the world's desperate needs.

As a specialist in computer simulations and as a founding organizer of the associations of computer simulationists both in Japan and in the United States, he asked why powerful computer instruments could not be used for "peace games" as well as for huge "war games," as by the Pentagon. When some people scoffed at the idea, he conducted demonstrations: for example, connecting experts in Tokyo, New York, Honolulu, and the Vancouver World's Fair for "computer assisted negotiations" to prevent a world crisis. He persuaded a United Nations official, on his own time, to prepare a realistic scenario, and leading experts in U.S.–Japan negotiations to pay their own way to participate, using the FUGI computer model of the world (an illustration of a "global scale tool") and its data bases in the negotiations.

Utsumi found that a major barrier to such use of international computer networks, simulations, and telecommunications were the regulatory laws of different nations, which raised barriers in these "electronic highways of the future." So he founded the GLOSAS (GLObal Systems Analysis and Simulation) Association. Through it he has done the political work for deregulation, which has made it possible for business people, politicians, and educators to communicate via computer networking from country to country. This work as well makes possible his dream of interconnecting graduate schools in political science in various countries for "computer peace gaming."

He then began to turn his energies in the direction of using these "global-scale computer tools" to reform and empower education all over the world. His work in deregulation made possible the exchange of college courses between North America and Asia via computer networking, slow scan television, and live television on the NHK network in Japan. Thus students in Hong Kong and Singapore, for example, now take courses from universities in America via computer networks.

Why, he asked, shouldn't the parochial, nationalist, old-fashioned universities of the world be united, electronically and via computer networks, into a "global electronic university" that can offer anyone, anywhere in the world, the highest quality of education? There could be a great CD–ROM library on a satellite that any small school in a poor country could use. Utsumi cannot by any means claim credit for much that is happening today, as the world's universities are increasingly all interconnected with computer networks, as research scholars in many countries use computer networks and computer bulletin boards to work together daily. However, his restless insistence and persistent demonstrations of possibilities keep pushing others to their limits.

Utsumi is a member of the board of the "University of the World," which is incorporated to interconnect all the world's universities; and he is chairperson of the organizing committee for a Global University Consortium (GU), in process of formation. He is thus helping universities in Japan and in the U.S. to set up teleconference courses which can be taken jointly by students in both countries; and he has conducted the first official across-the-Pacific demonstrations of the combinations of technology which now make a "global electronic university" possible.

One reason Utsumi has been able to do things that other people saw as "impossible" or as "idealistic and premature" has been his continuing and thorough research. His expertise thus keeps him ahead of others and also earns a respect which makes it difficult for others to disagree with or to oppose his efforts. He is author of over one hundred scholarly papers, including "Peace Games with an Open Modeling Network" in S. Shoemaker, ed., *Computer Networks and Simulation III* (North Holland Publishing Co., 1986); and "The Emerging Global Electronic University" in *The American Journal of Distance Education*.

There is no reason, he says, why these "global-scale tools" cannot be used to try out and explore entirely new kinds of solutions to global problems, by simulating them without risk. He points to the successful use of computer simulations in breakthroughs accomplished in the United Nations "Law of the Sea" negotiations as an example. Utsumi isn't just talking about "compassionate uses of computers" or about the college history course taught jointly in Moscow and Boston in 1988–89, with students having the same lectures and readings, and with Russian and American students conducting class discussions electronically as if they were in the same room. Utsumi conducts one demonstration after another (in 1989–90, for example, negotiating to assist universities in America and Asia to offer such joint courses) to show what interconnected computers can do, in ways that are impossible to ignore or reject as "mere talk" and dreaming.

EXERCISES AND PROJECTS

1. *Bible Study*

Read Acts 2:1–2, the coming of the Holy Spirit at Pentecost.

What would or will be the equivalent of Pentecost in a mighty convocation of scientists and religious leaders seeking the power of the living God to redirect computer science? What are the "conditions" which must be satisfied by those who come together to seek such power?

Discuss: What is divine power revealed in the history of the church? Where does the power – needed to "do the impossible" of sending computers to all the places mentioned in this chapter – come from? See Psalm 150; and Mark 9:23, "Everything is possible to the one who has faith." What is the relationship between faith, praise, power?

2. *Theological Reflection*

Power to take computers where they should be going comes from God. The "people of God" need to have courage to seek and to claim that power. Such seeking and finding is the meaning of *worship* in the scientific age. In worship we seek God, and in our seeking, we find God. The *meaning of worship* for those who are taking computers where, theologically, they belong is: *the shared search for divine power* amd guidance *to do what must be done.* The people of God must not shirk their responsibility to bring their work and worship together to this end.

3. *Theological Reading*

To understand Christian teaching regarding the people of God, see H. Berkhof, *Christian Faith* (Eerdmans, 1986), chapters on "Israel" and "The New Community." On the challenge of being called, see Paul Tournier, *The Person Reborn* (London: SCM Press, and New York: Harper, 1975) and *A Place for You* (London: SCM Press, and New York: Harper, 1968).

4. *Exercises and Discussion*

(*a*) Who is presently sending computers where (theologically) they "should go"? Who should be sending them, and who (individuals and groups) are "called" to do this?

(*b*) Congregations: Appoint a team of reporters to discover where computers are going, and prepare a news report (in the categories proposed in this chapter) to be shared with the church at large. One group could monitor television programs, another radio, a third film, and a fourth newspapers. One subgroup could study non-fiction books, another periodical publications. A group of teenagers could watch films and science fiction stories. Reports on findings could be shared monthly at a church meeting, together with a library of videos from television.

(*c*) A church arts group might write science fiction about churches taking computers where they should go.

(*d*) Theological colleges and seminaries: Can the theological faculty of a graduate or undergraduate college undertake, for a period of years, to be a think tank searching into the divine redeployment of computers and related technology?

(*e*) Christian magazines: The editor announces a competition for the best news or fiction items about using computers for compassionate purposes, and to solve fundamental human problems.

(*f*) Youth groups: Appoint a commission of teenagers to study Asimov's collection of short stories (see further reading section at the end of this chapter). Ask them to discover, by study and prayer, the Christian counterpart to Asimov's "Three Laws of Robotics" which deal with how robots must not harm humans. For example, Matthew 25:31–46 could be titled "Christ's Laws of Robotics" – robots shall help feed the hungry, give drink to the thirsty and clothes to the naked, provide medicine for the sick, etc.

(*g*) Ask a children's group to make up a collection of children's stories about compassionate robots (= Helplots). Children should be encouraged to draw the "Helplots," paint them, model them, proposing a new industry parallel to robotics.

(*h*) Questions to organizations: Can I(we) learn to apply, quite systematically, the principles of problem solving and group problem solving to the following questions – How can my organization, church, or denomination send computers to where they should be going? What must change in our thinking about computers and God, Christ, church, religion? What is *crisis intervention* for the world of computers as approached from the world of religion? Who "owns" the problem of the world's needy and their relationship to the goals and direction of the "world of computers"?

5. *Prayers*

Give to our churches, O God, and to the world church, a "world mission media lab" where the formulation of mission theology – and of mission to the sciences – is integrated with computer-empowered study and new instruments for worship (such as computer art and music) as a place of discovery of both your will for the emerging computer age and of the power to heed your will and follow it.

Give to our mission theologians, O God, courage "boldly to go where no person has gone before" – to computers and their world. Give us young people – brilliant young scientists, engineers, artists – who will help our churches answer the divine question "Who will go for me?" with Isaiah's "Send me!" (Isaiah 6). And give to us theological teachers who will be masters of philosophy of science, so that these people can go, fully equipped with Christ's computers to do his great works.

Give to us, O God, a school of theology that will become a beacon of light to the "nations" of science and technology.

6. *Meditations*

Some theological students are asked by a teacher of early church history to "meditate on a saint a day." Would it be helpful in computer science, too, to reflect upon the biographies included here?

Let us imagine the "yet more glorious day" spoken of in the hymn "For All the Saints." Imagine that the son of man appears in great glory, the "saints triumphant rise in broad array," all the heroes and heroines of the church, of Israel, etc. Suppose they appoint us, our group, as their successors in the realm of computer science. As we meditate upon their lives, seeking inspiration of moral excellence and responsibility in *relation to the world of computers*, we can experience the "church militant on earth" as assisted by the "church triumphant in heaven" in the guidance of mission in relation to computers.

7. *Worship Suggestions*

Call to worship: Use the above paragraph.

Bible study: Acts 2.

A presentation of news of people who are taking computers where they should go.

A recollection of God's actions in history (for example, Elijah against the prophets of Baal, I Kings 18) and sermon on finding divine power through praise and repentance.

Offertory of all existing initiatives in which computers are going to the places this chapter identifies.

Holy Communion to consecrate lives dedicated to mission with computers.

8. *Suggestions for Further Reading*

On robots see Isaac Asimov's collections of science fiction, short stories – *I, Robot* (New York: Doubleday, 1984) and *The Rest of the Robots*. See also Grant Fjermedal, *The Tomorrow Makers* (New York: Macmillan, 1989) in which a reporter goes to major theologians to ask theological questions about robots and finds them, for the most part, unprepared to answer.

On the theory of problem solving see Rod Napier and Matti K. Gershenfeld, *Groups: Process and Theory* (Boston: Houghton Mifflin, 1984). For a transactional approach, see the paperback text in transactional analysis, by Muriel James and Dorothy Jongeward, *Born to Win* (New York: New American Library, 1978).

On Bonhoeffer, the major text is edited by Eberhard Bethge, *Letters and Papers from Prison* (London: SCM Press, and New York: Macmillan, 1970). Bethge's *Dietrich Bonhoeffer* (New York: Harper and Row, and London: Collins, 1970) contains an important section on his critique of religion. Also *I Knew Dietrich Bonhoeffer*, Wolf-Dieter Zimmerman and Ronald Gregor Smith, eds. (London: Collins, 1973).

On the study of worship see Cheslyn Jones, et al., *The Study of Liturgy* (London: SPCK, 1983).

On computers going into education, medicine, the Third World, global problem-solving, etc., see Pamela McCorduck, *The Universal Machine: Confessions of a Technological Optimist* (New York: McGraw Hill, 1985).

NOTES

1. *PC Computing* (November 1988), 44.
2. See M. Turoff et al, *Computerized Conferences and Communications Center* (Newark: New Jersey Institute of Technology, 1980).
3. Here Ted Nelson's *Computer Lib/Dream Machines* is very helpful, as well as his own research.
4. See, for example, Stuart Bremer, *Simulated Worlds: A Computer Model of National Decision-Making)* (Princeton: Princeton University Press, 1977); also H. Guetzkow and J. Valadez, *Simulated International Processes* (Newbury Park, Calif.: Sage Publications, 1981).
5. See, for example, the book *Balance of Power: International Politics as the Ultimate Global Game* (Redmond, Wash.: Microsoft Press, 1986) about the computer game of the same title and its creation.
6. *New Options Newsletter* (April 1985).
7. See T. Utsumi, P. Rossman, et al, "Peace Games With an Open Modeling

Network," in S. Shoemaker, *Computer Networks and Simulation III* (Amsterdam: Elsevier, 1986) and "Waging Peace with Globally Inter-Connected Computers" in H. Didsbury, *Challenges and Opportunities: From Now to 2001* (Washington, D.C.: World Future Society, 1986). The United Nations "Law of the Sea" negotiations also demonstrated a process greatly facilitated by a computer database and simulations, as reported in P. McCorduck's *The Universal Machine* (New York: McGraw Hill, 1985).

8. Prof. L. Weed of the University of Vermont Medical School has experimented with and demonstrated such comprehensive medical records. The quality of medical care all over the world has been improved by computer network connections to research data bases, and the American Medical Association has reported plans for an earth-low orbiting satellite which, at low cost, can extend such connections to some of the most impoverished areas of the world.

9. See P. Rossman, *Computers: Bridges to the Future*, chaps. 3 and 8 (Valley Forge, Pa.: Judson Press, 1985).

10. For many other parish uses of computers, for example, in evangelism or in the creation of "Talent Banks," see K. Bedell and P. Rossman, *Computers: New Possibilities for Personalized Ministry* (Valley Forge, Pa.: Judson Press, 1984).

11. See Alfred North Whitehead, *Religion in the Making* (New York: New American Library, n.d.).

12. Alfred North Whitehead, *Science and the Modern World* (New York and Cambridge: Cambridge University Press, 1938), 238–39.

13. See A. R. Peacocke, *God and the New Biology* (London: Oxford University Press, 1989).

14. Such an initiative is a central concern of the World Network of Religious Futurists, which is conducting conferences on such topics.

4

Compassionate Computers – Ways They Could Help

Alongside the created term "computer," we ask if today's prophets should not call for a new term and for the creation of "machine/software" invented and governed (in its computer programming) by compassion. Tongue in cheek, we will call this a "computer for human need" or a "compassioner."

Why a compassioner? The prophets of ancient Israel served their nation in many ways. One was to lead a kind of national repentance and "theological reflection." As partners with the priests they led people in a search for God's will and ways to discern the meaning of events in their national life.

As we contemplate the social and justice-related crises associated with "the world of computers," one biblical seer is especially relevant – the prophet Joel. We are reminded of the scientists who today warn of ecological disaster – desertification and deforestation, the depletion of the ozone layer, the poisoning of the seas – when we read Joel's appeal (chap. 3) for a mighty conclave in response to the national catastrophe. He summons the entire populace to a great "moot" or parliament, a "town meeting" of the people.

In a time of supreme crisis, the most valued assignments of role and function in society must be suspended: the priests must leave their altars, the honeymooners their bridal chamber, the children their schools and play. The existing chambers of congress and commerce, the "structures of church and state," and the well-established scientific societies must at least temporarily be abandoned. Sinners and saints, the wise and the innocent, the jokers/comedians and the solemn judges now forget their class/role distinctions. The beggars at the gate must also rush to the great confabulation, for no possible resource can be neglected.

Then, as now, the prophet blew the trumpet to announce a time of overpowering crisis.[1] Every citizen is summoned to come forward with ideas and energies. All must come at once or it will be too late. There may be no society left if the disaster is not dealt with promptly. And the assembly must begin with repentance, admitting human failures and weaknesses and a willingness now to move in new directions.

The prophet Joel's notion of an urgent sacred parliament contains an insight of timeless worth. In modern terms, we might say that Joel was setting up a global-wide computer-network think-tank so that every resource of society could be brought to bear on the crisis and its resolution. When a crisis or catastrophe of mind-numbing magnitude is at hand, all of human society's resources must be mobilized, especially the creativity and intelligence of many minds. If necessary, they are to think the unthinkable. That is, they may shatter the "rules of thought," such as the divisions between sciences or the conventional quest for "objectivity." They will be more open to ingeniousness and childlike faith, the unspoiled ideas of youthful freshness, to minds "naive" enough to have hope and vision.

We do not know what the prophet Joel would say if he came again in our time. We would not be surprised if he warned us that we live at a moment of terrible crisis. He would, we suspect, warn us that a body – such as the earth or the human community – cannot be healthy as long as half of it is sick (as seen in the illness and hunger of half the world's children). He would probably also point out to us that, for the first time in human history, we have the capacity to destroy all life on earth, all of humanity, and that we may indeed do so unless we repent (which means opening our eyes to see what is going on, for example, in the population explosion) so as to turn in a new direction.

What might he say to those who are in the "world of computers?"

A prophet like Joel would do much more than warn of dangers. He would also point to sources of motivation and power to prevent disaster. Perhaps he would again call for a mobilization of the best minds, for people to come together to search their hearts. To computer scientists, and those in the "world of computers" who have astonishing new power in their hands, he might call for a new kind of computer instrument: the "compassioner"; and he might call for leadership from such unlikely prophets as "futurists."

He would see computers and their world/industry neither as destroying pests (the locusts of scientific society), nor as invaders from an enemy nation or outer space. He would not see them as intrinsically evil or as intrinsically a social good, either. He would point out that good or evil can be magnified by computers, as was/is the case with nuclear energy, television and print, with electric motors and space exploration.

A prophet Joel, looking with fresh eyes at our world, would see the power of computers as highlighting the tragedy of the human condition. He would point to the galloping acceleration of computer power as representing a crisis in this respect: it reveals something of the power of God to solve human problems. Yet this power is not directly being used to reach out to the world's helpless, that underclass of miserably left out and neglected people. Surely a Joel would see this acceleration of computer power as an incipient judgment on contemporary society which, for example, has the power now to feed all the world's hungry children, to give adequate education and health care to all of them, yet does not do so. As computers are increasingly used to empower science, technology, economics, and politics, the prophet asks the following inescapable question:

> *How can this computer power be used with compassion, so that such caring can be placed at the very core of computer science?*

A Scenario

A prophet does not merely point a finger at evil and neglect, but also, often in symbolic and figurative speech, seeks to open the human mind to new possibilities. So, to stimulate the reader's imagination and vision, we suggest that a prophet like Joel would today call for another kind of "mighty conclave," summoning scientists and religionists (as voices for compassion) to a new dialogue, an urgent confabulation which might well be electronic, via computer networking.

A prophet like Joel would, of course, point to what is already going on in society rather than calling for something so entirely new as to seem discouragingly impossible. He might point to the way MacArthur Foundations funds are being used quietly, almost without notice, at the Center of Theological Enquiry at Princeton to bring scientists and theologians together for continuing conversations. He might point to the new society for religion and science in Europe, which is bringing together hundreds of leading scientists for talk with leaders of major world religions. He might point to the Order of the Academy of Christ which on three continents is seeking young people to educate themselves in both science and theology, as the Danforth Foundation-funded "Society for Religion in Higher Education" did in the United States.

Would the prophet then propose a scenario, or summon us to pick up on such trends to develop a plan for ourselves?

(1) Perhaps he would speak persuasively for a World Parliament of Science and Religion (to mobilize the resources of science and religion for the world's needy and to help motivate action in solving global crises). The call for such a parliament was made in 1988 by the emerging Network of Religious Futurists, an outgrowth of the World Future Society, and the American network of religious futurists which has been supported by the Joint Strategy and Action Committee of several major American religious groups. The suggestion has been made that such a parliament should not only be empowered by computer data banks and networking, but might also be the first such international assembly to meet continually across a number of years via computer networking. It would then be a *standing* world parliament of Religion(s) and Science.

(2) A prophet like Joel might urge a science-religion dialogue – an effort to bring heart and mind together – in order to create theologies in the major religious communities which are more adequate for a time when the political power of resurging world religions, especially fundamentalism in all of them, must be answered with a more effective use of human intelligence to serve the world's most desperate needs. On this point we will speak as Christians and what this might mean for one area of Christian theology: a new look at Christ's compassion.

(3) A Joel today might also call for some new imaginative combinations of technology which we are calling a "compassioner," especially designed for mobilizing the forces of religion, science, and compassion to serve the world's crises.

We will now look at each of these three prophetic possiblities.

The Scenario: A World Parliament of Science and Religion

The prophet who would call for such a global assembly could suggest that the time is ripe by pointing to the emerging history of parliamentary discourse, mature after centuries of experimentation. The work of the United Nations, the World Future Society, and so forth, have raised the consciousness of the human race to a geopolitical or transnational level. There have been parliaments of religion, indeed the Vatican and the World Council of Churches have quietly initiated dialogue among scholars of various religions and occasionally with scientists. The range of international scientific conferences is even more impressive. The World Forum held highly significant global conferences of parliamentarians and religionists at Oxford in 1988 and Moscow in 1989.

As yet, however, there has never been a truly global parliament of science and religion together, although the government of Costa Rica in 1989 invited scientists and leaders of all religions to a conference on ecology which would discuss a "Universal Declaration of Human Responsibility." In 1988–89 the World Network of Religious Futurists explored and experimented with a larger idea, proposing that each part of the world and each religious and scientific group should be free to respond within the "genius" of its own traditions.

In Europe, the form might be that of a standing Parliament of Science and Religion, perhaps as a prelude to exploring a true morally based world governing of science and technology. Walter Truett Anderson's highly recommended book, *To Govern Evolution*,[2] outlines an agenda of desperate need.

In America, the focus of a world conference of science and religion might be "practical," less institutional, focusing on ways in which the suffering and helpless people of the world might be directly helped. This idea has been furthered by the plans for, and followup after, the July, 1989, conference of the World Future Society in Washington, D.C., where leaders of five world religions were invited to report on how they might better help the world's suffering children, especially how they might use computer networking and technology to empower such action.

In Asia (as seen in such a conference in India, for example) the approach might be more meditative, influenced by Hinduism and Buddhism, to seek the divine center of science and technology, seeing science as a medium of revelation rather than of redemption.[3]

Such a "prophetic" proposal by a group of futurists is motivated by the weight or stress of the "world pain:" the horrific mass of suffering in the world and the way the "scaffolding" of religion is buckling under that pain. To some it seems as if the "bridge" from individuals to God, which religion heretofore has represented, is breaking up and a new one, based on compassion, must be formed.

One such prophet is Professor Earl D. C. Brewer of Emory University in Atlanta, Georgia. In 1986, in an article "A Religious Vision for the 21st Century,"[4] he called for a *United Religions Organization* "to provide vision and moral power through which other world-level organizations could function for the good of all." Brewer believes that a dialogue "among the world's major faiths could clarify and enhance global goals," and his plan encompasses science, or scientific issues, as well as religion. He calls for a "world level of debate about the critical issues – especially nuclear holocaust and starvation." The world Network of Religious Futurists, of which Brewer is now chairperson, also adds other critical moral issues to the agenda, especially the possible positive uses of computer science, robotics, artificial intelligence, supercomputers. A prophet like Joel might suggest that this may require a kind of sister organization to the United Nations, a branch of "world governance" in which the scientific and religious faculties of humankind come together to identify and seek to cope with issues long identified by the United Nations, but where progress has been slow.

How else than through dialogue conferences can compassion and science be brought together? Such organizations as Computers for Social Responsibility as yet fail to enlist and challenge major scientists because their eyes are concentrated on their scientific goals. As Dostoevsky graphically demonstrated in *The Brothers Karamazov*, in his story of the Grand Inquisitor, it is morally intolerable that even *one* child should suffer hunger and disease while the rest of the world has food and medical care. For Christians, this principle is at the heart of the faith, as seen in the Jesus' parable of the Lost Sheep (Luke 15:2–6/7) and in the Matthean vision of mission and christology (Matt. 25:31–46) which sees any suffering, neglected child as *being* Christ himself.

The rationale and method for a global science-religion conference should not be to ask how scientists and theologians agree or disagree, but should focus on crisis intervention, on meeting the need of the world's suffering children.

Another dimension of method is meditation, as portrayed with great brilliance in the future history of humankind in Olaf Stapledon's science fiction work, *Last and First Men* (1930), a text which can be studied as a treatise on human nature so as to provide inspiration.

A religious prophet (see Psalm 76) would again call for God to arise "to save the oppressed of the earth." For God "all things are possible" (Mark 10:27). There can be continuing breakthroughs in theology, religion, spirituality, as well as in the science of superconductors or in medical technology. The world's best prophets may be as yet undiscovered. One possible scenario: a theological college with a new "school for prophets" to revive the ancient prophetical guilds to live again in a new way.

Young people today might also get a vision of possibility from Tolkien's "Council of Elrond" in *Lord of the Rings*. That classic fantasy story opens with the discovery of the "Ring of Power," symbol of science and technology. This ring, made by the Dark Lord, Sauron, to control all other sources of power, has come into the possession of the friendly, comfort-loving hobbits or haflings. They don't know what to do with it! Their friend, the wizard-magician, Gandalf (symbol of the priestly-prophetic consciousness), escorts them to a great moot or council with Elf-Lord Elrond at his famous semi-magic residence "Lothlorien." The elves, dwarves, people, and hobbits there join Gandalf in pondering the riddle of the destiny of the Ring of Power. It cannot be wielded by them in their own causes, for it corrupts those who use it.

Consider: (1) They cannot take the Ring of Power (computer?). It must be unmade: it must be cast into Mount Doom. (2) Tom Bombadil (Lord and Symbol of "Unspoiled Nature") cannot do it. The ring is powerless over him; but in the end he too will fall, last as he was first. (A similitude of monasticism, or perhaps of Sir Galahad). This means that "Nature," that is, pre-scientific religion, cannot handle the problem of the world of computers. (3) Therefore they must think the unthinkable: (a) The ring must be returned to Mount Doom, that is, only computer science can redeem computer science, hence the "world brain" must have a "world heart" (empowered, we suggest, by compassionate computers). (b) The smallest and weakest must go to do it (hobbits = meek Christians?).

The Remaking of Theology

Many theologians, because they find it hard to keep up with science, say that they are poorly prepared and are therefore reluctant to engage in ongoing dialogue and conferencing with scientists – even for the most urgent of causes, that is, saving the human race from disaster.

We speak here to Christians, suggesting that while knowledge of science is important, the task of the theologian in the dialogue is now that of compassion. Christology, which has come a long way in its two thousand-year history, must now make a sudden leap forward.

Again, imaginative young people today might be helped to understand this task by reading the little-known science fiction short story, "Pusher,"[5] in which human beings discover their identity as a capacity to accelerate the spaceships of the Galactic Federation. Humankind is "Pusher," that is, responsible for scientific and moral acceleration. The story ends with the human being realizing his identity among the aliens so that: "Suddenly the ship surged forward at six times the speed of light. It continued to accelerate." This suggests what can happen to the Christian faith (focused in christology) when it truly finds itself among the needy (Matthew 25:31–46).

A leap forward in christology can take place – is taking place – along a number of horizons, all around the rim of contemporary theology. For example, the church – laypeople as well as theologians – is in many parts of the world beginning to see that the subject matter of christology is summed up in Matthew 25:31–46. One finds and meets Christ, one understands Christ in the discovery that he *is the little, needy, helpless ones*. Where they are, meeting their needs, is the empowering christology for our day.

Second, christology must be wrenched free from theology as intellectualism, theorizing, speculation, and argument. It must be given back to the people of God. Laypeople, including scientists, must be asked to think about God's love in Christ for our time, and in that context to reflect upon the meaning of their experience. But who has adequate time for that and how is it possible? Can empowering computer technology help?

Third, we make an audacious suggestion – one that will seem outrageous to many – that christology (and all other aspects of theological revisioning in our time) must be linked with computer science. This in some ways is the central theme of this book, and especially of this pivotal chapter. The enlarged christology which is needed to help motivate Christians in the world of computers, and of religion and science, *will come as global communities of scholars begin to work together*. This means C.I., collective intelligence, rather than A.I. artificial intelligence. And that collective task is now becoming possible as communication and computer tools are combined with all kinds of related technology to make it possible for human beings to undertake tasks – for corporate human service – on a scale that has never been possible before.

For example, no one theologian can cope with all of science, but a computer data-based *team* of scientist-theologians could. Ronald Weissman of the University of Maryland, in "From the Personal Computer to the Scholar's Workstation,"[6] tells how collaborative work can now take place among a global network of scholars and resources. Computer tools now exist for the organization, classification, and analysis of information, allowing the researcher to move into a world of integrated computing environments. A rich set of related tools makes it possible to store a lifetime of research notes, intelligently cross-referenced and interlinked, with access to image – slides and films – as well. In "The Great American History Machine,"[7] David Miller of Carnegie Mellon University describes such a computer workstation which can enable scholars to see patterns and to analyze what they see.

Emerging interdisciplinary scholarship and a great deal of the enlarging dialogue among religions in our time is possible because of such technology, as is much of the lay theology, involving scientists and others, which has become important in the religious life of this century.

A prophet such as Joel might next propose linking many of the world's theological colleges in a global computer network[8] so as to make possible mega-research projects in theology.[9] Theological schools which are related to universities can already be interconnected globally through computer networks such as Bitnet, as noted in John J. Hughes, *Bits, Bytes, and Biblical Studies*.[10] A Petronet – a global church network "piggy-backing" on such existing networking to interconnect congregations, research institutes, and human service projects all over the world – provides one clue to what a "compassioner" might be: new combinations of computer technology devoted to human service.

Computers for Compassion

We are not speaking simply of fundamentally remaking computers, which increasingly are involved in everything in society. We suggest that if the prophet Joel returned to earth today he might call for a new computer-empowered coalition of the religious futurists of all religions as a new world force, a new ray of the "world soul," a new burst of power for the "world heart," a "moral laser beam" of coherent light focused on the places of dark failure in contemporary society.[11]

Combinations of technology designed to use computer power compassionately would in part be a global communications system to make powerful new interconnectedness and relationships possible (the "world heart"), but it is envisaged as much more than technology. The "compassioner" needs energy and power, the energy of moral creativity, which in some ways can be compared with a vividness of imagery to a moral quasar; an act of God which is experienced in the senses as a sudden, crushing power at work (see Exodus 15:1–18), an initially incomprehensible, enigmatic, stunning outburst, as portrayed in Arthur Clarke's film, *2001: A Space Odyssey*, which was based on his short story "The Sentinel." There the sudden, bewildering "cry to the stars" was enacted by the mysterious Monolith.

The power needed by science and theology is that of an amnesty, the power to proclaim a "forgetting," a new beginning to transcend old squabbles, errors, and misunderstandings. Isaiah 40 tells of one such amnesty, and again and again the prophets have announced these, so that this history has its own trajectory.

Never before, however, has such an amnesty been announced with respect to science and technology. Now that step must be taken! What is to be forgotten in this asked-for amnesia? Old conflicts between religion and science; the past and present of computers, their history which so often forgot about morality. Perhaps there will be intermediate stages – "missing links" between computers and compassioners. The latter, indeed, may become the "archaeopteryxes" (species between birds and mammals) in the world of computers.

A true prophet, with an authentic vision from God, might also call for an "amnesty" in mathemathics so that a new era in the history of math can dawn, perhaps an era of "mathematical theology" and a "theology of mathematics" as a foundation whereupon compassion can be implanted in computer science, which is so closely linked to mathematical ideas. The linking of computers and compassion means going down into the "darkness" of foundations (basement) of the history of mathematical thought: for that is where computers came from. Perhaps psychoanalysts of math are needed for an understanding of how the basement of the human mind finds expression in mathematical ideas, especially "alienation."

A compassioner would, for example, be based on the "compassionate cosmological principle" which reveals the boundless, accessible love which God pours down into the cosmos wherever there are receptive human hearts, minds, and spirits. Thus kindness and generosity can be wedded with technology. In academic settings, philosophy of science (the "scientific outlook" and the "scientific method") can be governed by love of God and neighbor.

Computer Empowerment of Collective Intelligence

It is risky to suggest some of the technology that might come together in a "compassioner," or the new kinds of software programs which no one has yet envisioned. We would challenge those in the "world of computers," however, as well as scientists and theologians who may come together in an international conference, by pointing to some possible components of a "compassioner:"

First, global interactive data bases can bring together and make better use of all important information about major social issues and crises, such as millions of hungry children, and of the resources which can be organized and mobilized to meet such need, with imaginative cross-indexing and quick access provided by hypertext.

Second, the compassioner would include a global computerized communications network, such as those which already exist to serve business and military needs. One model is the world network for monitoring and warning about hurricanes and other such natural disasters, tied in with immediate information to relief and disaster service agencies. Such existing networks provide an important clue to structure of a "compassioner" which might make possible a networking of agencies of compassion for their mutual encouragement, empowerment, and effectiveness. Software and computer networking can empower a kind of on-line, research-and-action community.

Third, a compassioner can become a powerful instrument for meeting human need as it includes new computer tools for the arts and communications to seize the imagination of the public; for example, hypermedia, "desk top publishing," creative computer tools now available to artists, musicians, and inventors. Ted Nelson in *Computer Lib/Dream Machines* reports inspiring new art and music, films and videodisks that can transform and enrich human life. A "compassioner" to help generate *creativity* in many modes and guises may thus be born in a "media lab" where the experience of love, *koinonia*, and *shalom* can liberate human beings for inventiveness and transforming imagination.

Fourth, as the supercomputer is used for military accounting and record keeping of vast stores of weapons and ordinance scattered all over the world, as well as research, so also a "super compassioner" could monitor the resources that can make it possible to meet the needs of every child ("the least of these") on the planet, to make sure that none are neglected. It would now be possible to keep track of every child. Beyond Papert's "mind storms"[12] there should also be a proper diagnosis of each neglected child's needs, talents, deficiencies, etc. – not just medical – as the basis for a uniquely tailored education and care for each. Also education needs better instruments to create appropriate models as "goals" to use in evaluating progress of each and all, and tools that would help children develop in body and spirit, as well as intellectually.

Fifth, as computer science has been creating a Babel of "languages" and programs which are difficult for the average person to comprehend or use, humanity needs "unifying" languages and automatic translation programs. These can now begin to transcend the linguistic and ideological barriers which so often separate people. Such instruments help people share their ideas and manage problems and issues. In short, Babel can be replaced by communication and richer relationships. This would be the anti-Babel Pentecost of computer science.

Some additional components of a compassioner are suggested by some of its possible uses:

(1) We need "compassioners" to challenge or replace the emerging "computer priesthood" (those specialists who sustain secrecy, inaccessibility of the "mysteries" of their esoteric science). Publicly available knowledge can be made fully accessible so that people can help each other "in the full light of day" (Jesus said: all that is hidden will be made plain . . . and the honest person is not afraid of the light).

(2) Rightly used computers can help restore the beauty and integrity of the earth.[13] They can nurture human community, as well as the emerging global village. Mother earth (Gaia), in this way, can share her nourishment and gifts with the scientific community. By contrast, existing global-scale computer instruments are often used to pollute, destroy, and corrupt.

(3) Peace-gaming within the emerging global electronic university consortium can provide "star-peace" alternatives to technological war-planning. The geopolitical, military-industrial complex maintains weapons research, military testing, and arms buildup. Peaceable computer systems can tackle the global misery that is a fundamental cause of many of the wars in our time.

We suggest that the combination of outreaching love and computer science can thus generate moral vectors which, like heat-seeking missiles, search out the optimal ethical trajectory of strategic intervention in human suffering. The compassioner can help do the idea-processing and information management which can lead to the discovery of these ethical vectors: "critical path analysis" is here adapted to human needs, and can find its ethical fulfillment.

PROPHETS

James Clerk Maxwell (1831–1879), a physicist and devout Christian, initiated a far-reaching change in scientific understanding, paving the way for Einstein's theories. Born in Edinburgh, Maxwell was educated at Edinburgh and at Trinity College, Cambridge. He became the first professor of experimental physics at Cambridge in 1871. Earlier, in 1855, he had read a paper on Faraday's "lines of force" to the

Cambridge Philosophical Society. This foreshadowed his great work, *A Treatise on Electricity and Magnetism* (1873). He brought the kinetic theory of gases to a point where it remains identified with his name. Returning to Faraday's conception that all electrical and magnetic phenomena were stresses of a material elastic nature, he was able by the use of generalized coordinates to show that if the medium were identical with the so-called luminiferous ether, the velocity of light would be equal to the ratio of the electromagnetic and electrostatic units. This electro-magnetic theory of light is inseparably associated with Clerk Maxwell, and his theoretical work on electric waves suggested the experiments which have since developed into a system of wireless telegraphy.

It was Maxwell who found a conflict between "real connections in nature" and Newtonian theories based on "action at a distance." The behavior of electricity, magnetism, and light simply could not be explained in mechanistic terms. This forced Maxwell to break with Newtonian mechanics and to offer a very different explanation. This he did in terms of non-mechanical relations. He regarded these as immanent in nature. *He boldly unified electricity, magnetism, and light in a single theory.* He went on to develop the concept of the continuous dynamic field as an independent reality, which Einstein termed the most important change ever to have taken place in the logical structure of physical science.

When Maxwell published *A Dynamic Theory of the Electromagnetic Field* in 1864, Lord Kelvin wrote to tell him that in abandoning mechanistic models as scientific explanation he had lapsed into "mysticism." Maxwell had tried to restructure mathematics, calling for a new conception of "embodied mathematics."

Consider: Who will be the Clerk Maxwells of Christ-and-computers? How can we link intelligence and love as Maxwell linked electricity and magnetism? Who shall make such a linkage? How can the next generation be educated to make such a discovery? What are the implications for congregational life and theological education?

Note how Maxwell boldly rethought the basic ideas of his time. What needs to be rethought to lead the way to "compassioners"?

Robert Muller is a native of Belgium who grew up in Alsace-Lorraine. He holds degrees in law and economics from the universities of Strasbourg, Heidelberg, and Columbia (New York). During World War II he fought in the French resistance and was captured by the

Nazis. He has devoted his career since to international public service, performing diplomatic missions all over the world. He finally became Assistant Secretary-General of the United Nations in charge of the UN's economic and social services and the coordination of its thirty-two specialist agencies and world programs. In 1987–88, as a retirement career, he became the Chancellor of the experimental and imaginative United Nations University of Peace in Costa Rica, seeking to develop computer connections with Peace Research Institutes all over the world.

Muller is a devoted Christian with great vision: a true global, God-abiding political, moral, and spiritual renaissance to make our planet what "it was always meant to be: the Planet of God." In his book, *New Genesis: Shaping a Global Spirituality* (New York; Doubleday, 1984), he prays for "a new history . . . a new age, a new world . . . a new philosophy and new human relationships." He likes to say that, in order to have a better world, we must work at it, "we must be in love with it." When a missionary asked him how he could be so optimistic, Muller replied: "I am not an expert on optimism, you are! It is called the miracle of faith, the basis of religion."

His great dream, he says, is a "tremendous alliance" between the world religions and global politics as represented by the United Nations, to which he has given his life. He sees the United Nations not only as having been very successful in preventing disasters in the world, but as the world's greatest research center, a fact which most people overlook. In its computer data bases is a "wealth of knowledge on every conceivable world problem." Most of the increase in the world's people – from four and one-half billion to six billion by the year 2000 – will be poor people. Only with managed intelligence and more adequate research will it be possible to cope with the problems of population, environment, and natural resources that this will bring. The solutions lie in the realm of the spiritual, for humanity "has entered a totally new era."

He is optimistic because of the development of "an intricate . . . network of worldwide interdependencies" and *"collective thinking."* Few people see, he says, how humans are now cooperating on vast projects: "astrophysics and interplanetary science to solar science and outer space, the earth's atmosphere and its layers, the biosphere, the seas and oceans . . . the earth's surface and soils, the climate, the world's waters, energy . . . crust (minerals, underground water, heat oil), the bottoms of the seas, other living species, the microbial, genetic and planktonic world, the infinitely small realm of the atom . . . etc."

He tells how a "complete Copernican tapestry" is thus emerging, taking stock on an all-planetary scale of this total knowledge. The instruments by which all nations are able to cooperate on such ventures, he says, mark the beginning of a science of planetary management.

Muller is not only now giving leadership to global computer interconnections for peace and research, but dreams also of a great global celebration for the year 2000, "A Worldwide Bimillennium Celebration of Life" to bind the human family together. He writes of his colleagues of various religions at the United Nations who meet at the U.N. to design a better future for the world. Thus, he says, an increasingly united humanity, seeking its oneness, seeking justice, is composing, little by little, "a planetary prayerbook," seeking no less than reunion with the divine.

In *New Genesis*, this oustanding global statesman has a chapter on "Of Science and Love." He tells of a famous scientist who asked him, "What on earth has science to do with love?"

Muller gave him a long answer, saying: "Passion for life is the prime motive of scientific investigation. Human love for knowing and piercing the amazing creation is part of the process. Only love for the poorer people on the planet, and love for our entire beautiful planet, will allow us to find answers at the great conference on science and technology."

We have made great progress when it comes to knowledge about the human family, Muller says. In our great computer data bases are increasingly updated facts about who we are, where we are, how many of us are handicapped (ten percent of the world's children have a physical, sensory, or mental handicap by school age), malnourished (four hundred million), how many illiterate (a billion). To meet those needs, he says, the more we advance in science and technology, the more we will discover the "tremendous, simplifying, all-encompassing, meta-scientific virtues of love."

Humanity, this global politician says: "is ready for a new culture, which must include the benefits derived from meditation, prayer and spirituality." He says, "There is no reson why our planet should not be a floating cathedral in the universe. What better fate could we plan for?"

EXERCISES AND PROJECTS

1. *Bible Study*

Colossians 1:15–20 can help us develop a christology of compassion and an understanding of the power of unlimited, rule-breaking (gospel) love/compassion:

– the power to invent:

– the power to engage in transformative, "emergentive" creativity;

– the power to convert hearts and "raise the dead" (transform and make disciples);

– the power to give light, heat, strength;

– the power to give new kinds of energy beyond our present understanding of the electro-magnetic spectrum;

– the power to reach all people in many ways, some even as yet unguessed.

Discuss: How was the universe created? How do things come to their proper place or destiny? Does this apply to computers? How did God bring the universe back to God (verse 20)? What does this mean for computers?

2. *Theological Reflection*

We sing in Charles Wesley's hymn: "Jesus thou art all compassion, pure unbounded love thou art." It is Christ who is the cosmic principle of compassion. The universe has a divine core of love, its true center. From that core, that "singularity," came Christ: "Peace on Earth, good will toward men" (Luke 2:14). No limits can be sent to the magnitude of compassion pouring down from that divine center. Only the human capacity to receive can hinder the infusion of love (James 1:17). With compassionate computers – or "compassioners" – we can give practical expression to this divine, limitless compassion at the heart of science and technology. To receive this compassion into one's own being is the work of Christian meditation and contemplative prayer. To receive its transforming power into one's church/fellowship/congregation/community is the task of true worship. To accept its power as the meaning and the very life of one's science and technology is to serve Christ in the world of knowing and culture-changing.

3. *Theological Reading*

Jon Sobrino, *Christology at the Crossroads* (Maryknoll, N.Y.: Orbis Books, and London: SCM Press, 1978); James Cone, *For My People* (Maryknoll, N.Y.: Orbis Books, 1984).

4. *Exercises and Discussion*

Teenagers: Write a science fiction story about a world in which "compassioners" are the main instruments of government.

Graduate students in theology: Construct a christology of computers.

Local governments: Can a government conference on science and religion, or computers and compassion, be held? For example, computers in the service of the community. Talk to town government officials.

Schools: At an annual computer week, hold competitions for the best essays, plays, videos, technology projects, etc., on compassionate use of computers. As in New Jersey, invite an "inventor in residence." Discuss: what should be the agenda for a world parliament of religion and science?

For scientist groups: What is your concept or idea of "news?" when you read a newspaper or watch the "news," what are you subconsciously looking for?

What would be "good news" in the context of the convergence of compassion and computers? What would be a sensation? What would be a most-desired "exclusive" story concerning compassionate computers? (Compare the sensational conference in New York at which the breakthrough in superconductors was announced; or the Manhattan project.) List other scientific sensations in journalistic history.

Begin to devise an imagined, ideally desirable future news scoop about a breakthrough in the field of science and compassion, focused on certain actions/inventions/discoveries concerning computers. Then formulate prayers, then educational policies, which will bring that event closer.

5. *Prayers and Meditations*

A prayer using phrases from prayers of Robert Muller, former associate Secretary-General of the United Nations:

O God, forgive my multitude of words which are so feeble to express the greatness of your creation. Humanity has achieved such marvelous successes through science and technology, unlocking many secrets and mysteries of the universe, providing longer and better lives and improved knowledge for large numbers of people. Now, as we are entering a new age, we must make a giant leap into the future, and there is a pressing need to bring into full play the forces of the "mystery of faith." For now must dawn a worldwide era of supreme reverence for all, for all our human family. We must define a new world ethics, respecting and loving each other. Help us to become a global family, endowed with common institutions: a common brain, heart, and soul, geared to human flowering on planet earth.

Whenever I am sad or in despair or in rebellion against the state of human affairs, I need but to think of you, O God, and all becomes bright again. "He who follows me," said the Christ, "walks not in darkness, for he will have the light of life." You, as a great, simple, limitless power, an all-encompassing mind, an all-embracing heart are as alive and indispensable today as at any other period of our human journey. You are the answer to our anxiety, the light in our darkness, the image of our future. I am in exultant joy before the magnificence of your creation.

For consideration: Psalm 76:1–2. The Lord breaks the bow and shatters the spear; *he breaks the flashing arrow.* (God can "square the circle".) This God, the *Ens Realissimum*, can shatter the trajectory of computer science and make it anew. God can make new arrows: the arrows of compassion-in-science. This God is now doing, as around the world the people of God sink deeper and deeper into meditation on the suffering world's children.

How can I/we support/share/enable/catalyze/expedite such pan-terrestrial meditation?

6. *Worship Suggestions*

Call to worship: use the paragraph above.

Bible study: Colossians 1.

Presentation of news of compassionate breakthroughs in computer science and robotics technology.

Intercessions for inventors and all kinds of social "imagineers;" prayers for organizations which fund/support research in scientific frontiermanship.

Sermon on the cosmic Christ and the Lord who breaks the flashing arrows.

Offertory of self and ideas, intentions about compassioners. Holy Communion to consecrate lives dedicated to discovery of scientific and metaphysical principles such as will promote the discovery of compassioners.

7. *Suggestions for Further Reading/Viewing*

Arthur C. Clarke, *Profiles of the Future* (London: Pan 1962) is vital reading for those who want to know the "hazards of prophecy," for example, the failures of "elderly but distinguished scientists" to predict space travel, etc. Helps us realize the value of unfettered imagination.

J. R. R. Tolkien, *Lord of the Rings*, vol. 1 (London: Allen and Unwin, and New York: Houghton-Mifflin, 1959). See the chapter on the Council of Elrond.

William Broad, *Star Warriors* (New York: Simon and Schuster, 1985), an account of the Livermore Laboratory in California where young physicians of genius have been seeking, in an operations research framework, principles by which breakthrough can be obtained in the star wars technology (SDI defensive shields, laser research, etc.).

John Passmore, *One Hundred Years of Philosophy* (Harmondsworth and New York: Penguin Books, n.d.), is a good introduction to the study of the ideas of the foundations of mathematics; advanced study can be undertaken in Morris Kline, *Mathematics: The Decline of Certainty* (New York: Oxford University Press, 1980).

J. Van der Veken and E. Lippens, *God of Change: Process Thought and the Christian Doctrine of God* (Leuven, Belgium: Center for Metaphysics and Philosophy of God, 1987). This book is a collection of articles from special issues of *Word and Spirit: A Monastic Review* (on process theology) and *New Blackfriars* (God and change).

The film *Things to Come* (1936) by H. G. Wells, starring Raymond Massey. See the final five minutes on the necessity of doing the unthinkable, on the necessity for the human spirit of progress into the beyond.

NOTES

1. As the economist Robert Theobald is doing today in his book *The Rapids of Change* (Indianapolis: Knowledge Systems, Inc., 1987).
2. (New York: Harcourt Brace, 1986).
3. Note Western scientists, such as F. Capra, who are led in this direction by contemporary physics and biology.
4. See *The Futurist* (July–Aug. 1986), 14ff.
5. Anthologized in *Contact*.
6. *Academic Computing* (October, 1988).
7. *Ibid.* Also of interest is "Relationships and Tasks in Scientific Research Collaboration" in D. Greif, ed., *Computer Supported Cooperative Work* (San Mateo, Calif.: Kaufman Publishers, 1988).
8. One British proposal calls it "Petronet." A computer network of theological schools is being discussed in Southeast Asia.
9. See *Computers: Bridges to the Future*.
10. (Grand Rapids, Mich.: Zondervan, 1987), 491.

11. The World Soul (*Anima Mundi*) is considered by Jungian psychologists to be psychologically real, at least as an archetype of the collective unconscious. The book *The World of Hinduism* defines "Brahman" (the Supreme Being beyond all attributes) *as* the "World Soul".

12. S. Papert, *Mind Storms* (New York: Basic Books, 1980) proposed entirely different uses of computers for children in education to stimulate thought and creativity.

13. See W. T. Anderson, *To Govern Evolution* (New York: Harcourt Brace, 1987), 332ff., on a great project to "restore the earth."

5

Christian Mission To Those Involved With Computers

Bishop Lesslie Newbigin, in such books as *Foolishness to the Greeks*,[1] discusses the Christian mission to the post-modern world – the world of technology and computers. This world, which is not just "Western culture," is increasingly shared by the educated leaders of all the world's cities and universities. To some extent he sees this new culture as a "whole way of perceiving, thinking, and living."

Newbigin served many years in India, another culture, very different from the Christian West. There he had to give his energy to the transmitting of the gospel from one culture to a radically different one. Now he asks if this modern scientific age is not also a radically different culture, a new "cultural frontier" facing Christians.

Since returning to England from India, his teaching and research at Selly Oaks Colleges, as a highly influential theorist, has focused on this question of missiology or strategy. He draws upon and acknowledges the great work of earlier twentieth-century theologians who analyzed the relationship between Christian faith and culture. He praises the work of Richard Niebuhr, whose book *Christ and Culture* proposed five models, or alternative possibilities, of relationship; and of Paul Tillich, whose life work continued the title of his first public lecture: "Theology of Culture." Newbigin adds to their work a firsthand experience on the boundary between two radically different cultures, such as he experienced in India. His experience there helped him to identify the problems involved in transmitting the gospel to the cultural world of modern science and technology.

Newbigin does not merely propose "dialogue" in a neutral sense, but the need to plan a missionary encounter between the gospel of love and "modern scientific culture."[2] This, however, is a very difficult task. Some would say that it will be hard because many scientists and computer people have closed their minds to religion, or at least the kind of institutional religion they have experienced.

The real problem, however, may be in the minds and hearts of those who seek to transmit the gospel to them.

What can we learn from the experience of those who have sought to carry the gospel to other radically different cultures? The Christian theory of mission has struggled for decades with the relationship between the "good news of Christ's love" on one hand, and the nature of "cultures" receiving – and *transmitting* – that message on the other hand. These studies have learned a certain modesty about the role of those who would seek to convey the gospel. It has to be expressed by the personality, life style and communication ability of the "missioner." So to that extent it cannot be "pure," but always carries with it at least the husk (and perhaps the seed) of the missioner's own culture. For example, when a missionary in rural India or Africa uses a radio, he/she is conveying the trappings of Western culture, and not just the gospel. Without wishing or intending it, she/he thus promotes a Western Christ and culture.

The dignity and integrity of various human cultures has required the theorists of mission – which in theology is a kind of science in its own right – to the task of more carefully separating the gospel, the good news of redemptive love, from all of its cultural trappings. Otherwise people in other cultures may be prevented from hearing and responding to the "good news of love." In many cases foreign cultural trappings may do damage to a culture.

It is therefore in this context that we reflect upon a "loving" mission to and within scientific, high-tech culture, and especially to its sub-culture, the "world of computers." We can profit from a "ripening" maturity of understanding about cultures and the nature of "Christian mission" itself, its main ideas and purposes. The Christian mission, theologically, is the presentation of the good news, or gospel of Jesus Christ to persons and peoples (Greek: *ethnai*) or civilizations. The concept of *peoples* can be interpreted to mean any self-contained sociological community, such as a science, a technology, an art, a religion, a well as sovereign state or tribal culture.

We should note, though, that even the *concept* or idea of the gospel is "culturally conditioned." The very idea of "good news" is Hebrew –Greek in origin. Bishop Newbigin believes that there cannot be, and never has been, a "gospel that is not embodied in a culturally conditioned form of words." He asserts that[3] "There can never be a culture-free gospel." Yet he goes on to say that "the gospel," which from beginning to end is embodied in culturally conditioned forms, *calls into question all cultures, including the one in which it was originally embodied.*[4]

What is the *result* of the impact of the gospel on a culture? The gospel of love is a kind of cosmic force – like light or heat – or perhaps intelligence. It changes, has the capacity to transform, wherever it impacts: it converts and heals, judges and illumines, redirects, sanctifies, opens to God. Theoretically it is the Holy Spirit, sometimes known as the "Go-Between God," who is the agent of this work, which in theology is called redemption, salvation, conversion, and sanctification.

So much for theological jargon. Can this be put simply? It can. This cosmic power of the gospel is basically a simple thing. It is *love*, unconditional love, appreciation, recognition, compassion, the healing power of affection, of touch. It is goodness expressing itself as outreaching, intelligent kindness.

This love is like "white light." A kind of theological spectroscope would reveal it to be made up of a number of constituent elements, each expressing an attribute of God: creativity, honesty, kindness and compassion, intelligence, courage, gentleness, goodness, forgiveness and mercy, all wrapped up in a single ray or beam of the power of God's love. Mission is the conveyance of this beam to others, to individuals and their cultures.

Following this imagery, we can postulate the psychological and political relevance of this ray. If we imagine a lighthouse, with its powerful revolving beam, we can consider the light of Christ to be a comparable ray – of love and spiritually illumined intelligence. The "people of God," the agape-illumined minds of the world, whether or not they are nominally Christian, seek to operate this lighthouse and direct its rays towards one people and then another. We write here to suggest turning this "ray" into the "world of computers" to throw some light of query and challenge into that high-tech milieu.

However, before we look at the people to be influenced or challenged in that world of computers, we ask *who* are to be the agents of mission to what, for some, must be like a distant planet. Newbigin poses this question in two ways.

Who Will Undertake the Mission?

(1) "From whence comes the voice that can challenge this culture on its own terms?" Newbigin first asks, not without some poignancy. "A voice

that speaks its own language and yet confronts it with the authentic figure of the crucified and living Christ so that it is stopped in its tracks and turned back from the way of death?" (see note 15).

Newbigin, himself, challenges this culture on its own terms. The voice which can be heard in the community of modern science must come from Christians who have specialized in modern science – including high-tech science – as well as in missiology. People with such qualifications need to be identified, commissioned by church agencies, and equipped for creative work. This must mean a partnership of "prophet and priest," that is, between those who represent the center of religious society and those who have a prophetic call.

Such prophetic voices in our time may sometimes seem outlandish, on the margins of society as the biblical prophets often were, symbolically wearing the twentieth-century equivalent of the wild garb of John the Baptist, perhaps eating the modern counterpart of locusts and wild honey.

To speak of John the Baptist is to recall the Nazirite tradition of ancient Israel. The Nazirite was an important figure, one of the intermediaries between God and man/society. His life was to be a focus of power, like a magnifying glass whose curvature directs light to a point, so that flame can be kindled. Here again is the image of the "ray" to be directed into a community of society. The Nazirite was consecrated to God, pledging never to cut the hair, drink wine, and so forth, during the period of the vow. Such abstinences were intended to open the Nazirite to be at least partly filled with divine power. Such a vow could be taken for a limited period or for life. (The law for the Nazirites can be found in Numbers 6:2.)

We suggest that mission to the world of computers requires similar "dedicated" persons (the word also reminds us that the "dedicated" computer is one which is especially prepared to serve a specialized purpose). An alliance between modern-day "prophets" and "priests" (the church establishment) can address itself to the formulation of a new "vow of the Nazirite" to guide the conduct of those who seek responsibly to direct a ray of compassion into the world of computers.[5]

(2) Secondly, Newbigin asks: "From whence can the voice, not of doom, but of deliverance be spoken so that the modern western world can hear it as the voice of its Savior and Lord?"[6] (John 3:17).

Prophets, we suggest, including those who would speak to and within the world of computers, operate within the vehicle of their religion. All such vehicles need a "wheel" and an engine or power drive. The "wheel of religion," in the case of Christianity, is made up of axles, spokes, and rims. The axle consists of the missionary agencies, Catholic, Protestant, Eastern Orthodox, evangelical, and councils of churches and denominations. The spokes of the wheel are the congregations, pastors and members. The rim is made up of missioners (as in the world of computers).

The engine which drives the wheel is the energizing vision and the will of the church's prophets. No small vision will be adequate to empower a mission to a scientific community. Such a mission, ideally, will also require the involvement of all the global agencies as well as an enlarging network of religious futurist-prophets. In global conferences which have brought together scientists and theologians, for example, we see glimmers of what is required: a "mega-vision" or "macro-mission." The book *Computers: Bridges to the Future* asked this question: Suppose new computer tools make it possible for us to do almost anything, what should Christians do in mission? A first answer was: We would wish for tools to help with research to understand the emerging computer culture, to help us clarify how to redesign the Christian mission for the emerging information age, for what Harvey Cox has called "a massive birth of spiritual energy."

In the last century, that book suggested, the mission boards of the churches had a "grand design," a comprehensive global strategy for the whole world: that is, to carry the gospel of love to every nation. Now we see that the "world" also contains strategic communities that are not geographic, such as scattered communities of researchers connected electronically in what is called "hyperspace." (Hyperspace is where people meet when, for example, they talk on long distance telephones.)

The question is not just where this voice of mission comes from. It is also a question of who will undertake the mission. We recall how, in the last century, John R. Mott, a young student who was headed for a brilliant political career, was recruited to be part of the original "missionary hundred" at a conference of the most outstanding students in American universities. Mott, later a founder of the YMCA and the World Council of Churches – went to universities all over the world at the turn of the century successfully to recruit the most talented young Christians he could find for his vision of the world mission. He called for the best to go on pioneering mission, and for all others to support them. So now some are suggesting a call for a "missionary thousand" to go into the scientific community.

In a sense[7] the church's global mission has been a kind of laboratory for experimentation, often establishing the first schools and colleges, the first agricultural experimentation stations, the first research hospitals. The mission to the world of computers will at least be this. Tools to facilitate partnership can now help people in many areas of work to share in the adventure and excitement of a larger vision, a quest for spiritual empowerment to improve the quality of people's lives along with the quality of their work. Human society faces overwhelming problems – for example the pollution of the environment, war, hunger, disease like AIDS – which require "great new designs" – such as those new computer tools make possible.

The Christian mission to universities, as defined across a generation, has been seen to be a call for excellence, for integrity and honesty in research, for the university itself to enlarge its vision of itself and its opportunities for human service. Similarly, the Christian mission to any such community in modern society is first of all a call to vision, to creative and compassionate imagination (see chapter 7).

Researchers are now being empowered to do what has never been possible before. Collective teamwork – such as we see in the current explorations of outer space – can inspire us to envision and realize tremendous research and action projects: for example, to bring adequate food, health care, education, and the nurturing love of the gospel to *all* of the world's children in our lifetime.

Mission to the World of Computers

Such a task in the "world of computers" requires people, but it also needs a plan, a design. Its nature must be carefully thought out, documented, launched, monitored, and completed. In this sense it can be compared to space exploration or to a military expedition, needing tactics, troops, supplies, courage and endurance, and often some on-the-spot genius in generalship as well.

However, such an analogy should not be pressed too far. The nature of a mission to culture is not a battle but a healing. Such a mission seeks to bring love and compassion, coupled with understanding and moral leadership, rather than judgment or regulation. It seeks growth, a blossoming of creativity in the scientific community, a ray of vision to inspire service and healing for all of humanity.

Newbigin reminds us that a first essential for this kind of mission is that it must be in the language of the scientific culture itself. What we write here is an illustration of how difficult that can be. "Nurtured in one culture" and its theological language, Newbigin says, "The missionary . . . has to communicate the gospel among people of another culture, whose world has been shaped by a vision of the totality of things quite different from that of the Bible." A mission-to-computers team needs:

– to define the cultural "world of computers;"
– to learn its language;
– to communicate to its members from within.

This will require extensive research, training and various kinds of data bases. How else can the team speak to those who never come to church, or those who keep their church life totally separate from their work in the world of computers?

Theologically speaking, Christ is already there in the "world of computers." He is everywhere ahead of Christians, especially where there is human need. If such a team is to meet him there in the world of computers and help others to do so, the team is called to live the gospel there in such a way that others can hear it in their own language, feel it in their own experience, and see it in the Christ who confronts them in their own world. Thus they can be suddenly grasped by his love, can understand it within computer science. Then his kingdom can grow there, as the whole loaf of bread rises after the yeast is placed within.

This book is offered to help Christians who are already there in the "world of computers," as well to help a support team of missioners such as we propose, to be clear about their call.

Before leaving Newbigin's rich and profound scheme of "mission to culture," we note his discussion of science and the sciences. In *What Can We Know: The Dialogue with Science* (his chapter 4), he provides material which can help a mission team in the encounter with the truth-claims of the philosophy of science (and math). Its self-image as "scientific" (that is, good and true) is an important part of the outlook of computer science. In chapter 7 we will discuss the claims of the gospel (moving beyond present understandings of philosophy of science) in relation to ideas of computer science *as science*.

Proposal for a Hyper-Mission

How then can we describe a more adequate Christian mission to those involved with computers?

First, we call the missioners "theological computer scientists." They will be found in congregations, in campus religious groups, in seminaries and graduate schools. Creative ways of finding and inviting such candidates need to be devised, for example using computer bulletin boards and user groups. Another strategy would be to work within existing religious orders, persuading some young people to become "high-tech friars" with a slogan like: "have computer – will serve."

The planning of such a mission and recruitment should involve people already in influential positions in the computer world, perhaps beginning by helping some of them recover and redirect their faith. A preliminary mission to them might be in the nature of a reconnaissance party, a pre-mission in which church leaders would seek to demytholo-gize computers.

A symposium in England on "Christ and the World Brain," and other such conferences, have found that many theologians and church leaders have a profound resistance to "getting involved with computers." It is almost as if they feel asked to go on a risky flight to outer space. So there is resistance on both sides of the needed dialogue. Certainly few of the leaders of the world of computers have been inviting religious leaders to participate in their planning and discussion, so as to keep compassion for the world's hungry foremost in their minds!

That resistance may be transcended as more thought is given to what should be done and how. An increasing number of religious leaders, and some theologians, are beginning to use computers, and a few even dare to talk about computer simulations and modeling as a way to explore new ideas and alternatives. As yet, however, very few[8] begin to use and develop computer data bases, or expert systems to manage information, or what we hopefully call "creative software" in the service of any Christian mission.[9]

So the first task is the development of the vision, and of the possibilities.

A Mission to the Ideas and Ideals of the World of Computers

The central ideas of the computer world include the basic scientific/mathematical concepts themselves, such as "computer," "world processor," program, "information technology." Secondly, they include the more speculative research ambitions of the computer scientist/philosophers. Some of these are actual research programs – the fifth/sixth generation computers which can translate from one language to another, for example. Others are general cultural ideals and often involve a certain vagueness: "thinking machines," "robots which are persons," and, half-way between dream and reality, "artificial intelligence," "world brain," and so-called supercomputers.

We propose three stages of mission to those concepts and ideals:

(1) To identify their underlying assumptions, so that these assumptions – philosophical, including metaphysical, and ideological – can be brought into consciousness. In other words, the underlying ideas and ideals presuppose and express convictions about what *is* the case (metaphysics), and what *should* be the case (ethics). It is very helpful to encourage computer thinkers to externalize these assumptions. This helps them to think more consciously about their own ethical system and its relation to the crises facing the world's people (and children) in our time. The enterprise of consciousness-raising about cultural ideals is central to Dan Beeby's "Gospel and Our Culture" program (in Britain) which is based upon Newbigin's books. It resembles an enterprise of psychoanalysis in which the psychologist helps the analyzand discover that confused or immature thinking patterns may unconsciously be guiding adult behavior.

(2) The assumptions and ideals which have been uncovered by this exercise are then compared with the cultural ideals and ambitions implicit in the gospel of Christ. We have already discussed what some of those compassionate possibilities are.

(3) By an effort of creative imagination (and for this phase, plenty of science fiction enthusiasts should be around), more suitable ideals and programs can be proposed to the computer world. For example, some scholars who have studied the computer "world brain" idea now seek to devise an alternative: the "world heart" network. Similarly, the possibility of using highly powerful new computer tools and networks to help people work together collaboratively, suggests that "collective intelligence" – which empowers human beings to put their minds together for more powerful thinking – may in our time be a more useful in the service of compassion than the quest for "artificial intelligence" in which computers can do our thinking for us.

Mission to the Technology

If we continue conventional understandings of mission, we will think of it as addressing only the persons involved with computers, and not the technology itself. Can we enlarge our vision to think of a mission to the technology also?

Yes, if we think of mission to the technology as involving two phases: the deployment of existing technology for more compassionate and just purposes, and the diversion of the course of research and development into a more compassionate and visionary direction, so that future technology serves God and human need more positively and directly.

Such a diversion calls for Christians who are willing to ponder the facts of computer technology, software, hardware, and associated ideas/ideals, and then to pray for the inspiration of the Holy Spirit in discovering concepts of technology, and actual software programs which are more directly geared to compassion. Our times call for world citizens who are equally adept in meditation and high-tech creativity – in the pleasures of spiritual discovery, through the grace of God, as well as the delights of technological invention.

To say this simply: We propose that the ideas and practices, the workplaces and training programs, the ethical codes and the very choice of materials and shape of products in the computer world be guided by charity and compassion. That is, by a desire to help the needy and in Anderson's understanding of ecological need, "to govern evolution."[10] Thus a radical transformation can take place, not only in the philosophy and educational practice associated with technology, its invention and deployment, but also in the hardware and software itself. For the skeptic we offer some examples.

On the compassionate side, we note how Stephen Hawking, the great Cambridge physicist who has Lou Gehrig's disease, can speak clearly for the first time in twenty years with the aid of a computerized speech synthesizer.[11] So much more like this could be done, like the child who cannot talk but who is now writing a novel on a computer, if only the public would "wake up" to what computers can do.

Not only handicapped persons, but handicapped churches can also be empowered. The American book, *Bits, Bytes and Biblical Studies*[12] reports on many computer-empowering tools, including "Gutenberg Sr.;" the Duke Language Toolkit; PowerWriter, created at Westminster Theological Seminary; Word Start/Hebrew; and others. One of the most significant is IBYCUS Scholarly Computer, a specially designed computer and software which is a remarkable religious tool. It makes possible high speed search through ancient texts with up to fifteen "windows" and four thousand and ninety-six unique characters on screen. It has multi-lingual word processing, combinable with CD–ROM – that is the technology that can store an entire encyclopedia on one disk – and laser printing technologies. This remarkable instrument is only a foretaste of what is now possible.

Many computer software programs for religious empowerment, starting as adaptations of programs developed for business or in education, are gradually improving and enlarging into a veritable library. Victor Lim, a British computer entrepreneur, tells for example of Dr Ken Dean, a British Christian businessman who founded Evangelsoft, a computer software company. Alongside such entrepreneurs are young software engineers, like Jenny Day, creator of a computerized Christian education game which is an interaction between the Bible and the John Bunyan literary classic, *Pilgrim's Progress.*[13] She sees her work as a profound expression of her Christian faith. "Software engineering," she says, "is as much an art as a science."

"Project Goodware" in England is one example of "mission to technology." It is designed to be a mission to the whole software industry – ideas, ideals, products, and methods of work. As "software" refers to computer programming and its electronic embodiment, and "wetware" is a term used by programmers for the human brain, so "Project Goodware" is a many-layered investigation of the content of computer programs, their methods of production, and the invention/production of responsible alternatives.

The "good" in its title refers to the good news, the gospel, for the program hopes to present the good news to the industry. Project Goodware, historically, is probably the first example of a plan systematically to evangelize an entire industry.

(c) "Mission" to the *practitioners* is pastoral, compassionate, and scientific. Presentation of the "good news of God's love" can be undertaken by individual Christians (including youngsters) or by groups of Christians. "Groups" can refer, for example, to congregations, mission boards, committees of bishops, societies of Christian computer scientists. For instance, some Christian congregations now twin with congregations or groups of needy people in other countries. It would also be possible, however, for all the congregations in a district to divide up the world of computers between them and to "twin" with branches of the computer industry.[14]

Suppose congregation "A" monitors and challenges "supercomputer research," congregation "B" does the same for "room temperature superconductors," and congregation "C" follows research in robotics and visits centers of design as well as factories which produce robots. In the denominational headquarters of these three congregations, the prophet Joel might envision a technological "missioner" who helps match congregations with sciences. Mission by the congregation involves monitoring the research and its aims, visiting the scientists and dialoguing with them and praying for their growth in compassion.

Such a mission to computer scientists can result in their turning from a style of thought and science which is largely profit-oriented to an outlook in which their passion is the search for a just world order – a search in which computers play a vital part in the accelerating outreach of human empathy and divine love.

A mission to the "philosophers of computer science" might involve the nurturing of a young cadre of Christians which would be divided into teams.

One team, for example, might prepare itself for visits to get acquainted with and then share research with computer journalists; another with media analysts; a third with professional philosophers of science. The preparation of such teams, as any religious enterprise, should be set in the context of worship. It is a ministry which should be commissioned in prayer. It has to be lived in the power of the Holy Spirit. So we conclude this point by calling attention to the "spiritual exercises and projects" which are at the end of each chapter in this book: Bible study, material for reflection (including science fiction novels and films), prayers, and questions for thought or group discussion.

MISSIONERS

Lesslie Newbigin was born in the northeast of England, in Newcastle-on-Tyne, in 1909. He was educated in Reading, and then at Queen's College, Cambridge. For two years he was Intercollegiate Secretary of the Student Christian Movement in Glasgow, and he spent the next three years at Westminster College, Cambridge. He was ordained in the Church of Scotland in 1936 and then went out to India to the Madras mission of his church, where he served until 1947, mostly at Conjeeveram. During two intervals at home he worked as Candidates Secretary for the Church of Scotland's Foreign Missions Office.

In 1947 when the denominations united to form the Church of South India, Newbigin was appointed Bishop of Madhurai and Ramnad. So it was as a bishop that he attended the First Assembly of the World Council of Churches at Amsterdam in 1948. In 1957 he became General Secretary of the International Missionary Council, and then served in Geneva as Director of the Division of World Mission and Evangelism of the World Council of Churches. During these years he traveled widely, including a time in South Africa.

In 1965 he returned to India as Bishop of Madras, in the Church of South India, and then retired to England in 1974. He began a new career in retirement, serving as Moderator of the United Reformed Church in England, 1978–79, and on a five-year term as a missiologist on the staff of the Selly Oak Colleges in Birmingham – a federation of nine colleges which train people for Christian education and missions. In his late seventies he accepted a call to be pastor of a small Reformed congregation on the outskirts of Birmingham, where he continues to write influential theological books. Two, written since he was seventy, have been *The Other Side of 1984* and *Foolishness to the Greeks*. The latter is a brilliant call for "mission to modern culture itself" and it resulted in an international mission program spearheaded by Dr Dan Beeby and the British Council of Churches: "The Gospel and our Culture."

Myron W. Krueger is a contemporary computer scientist who creates "responsive environments" which can sense human needs and respond to them. A professor at the University of Connecticut in the U.S.A., Krueger feels that computerized "responsive environments" provide glimpses of the future, as in education and forming global community.

He introduces his book *Artificial Reality* (London: Addison–Wesley, 1983) with references to Genesis, saying that a "new world has emerged" but "ironically we are profoundly ignorant of what we have made." The focus of his book is on the "interaction of people with machines" so that the computer perceives and responds to human behavior, amplifying the ability of people to interact with other people. Krueger's "artificial environments" are art forms, melding aesthetics and technology in a partnership between artist, computer, and participant.

As a result of computer technology, he says, we human beings are no longer creatures of only five senses; technology has given us hundreds. And as our computerized tools become more sophisticated, human beings are able to undertake tasks which are more and more ambitious. Simulations – such as simulations of moon landings in advance – are a form of computer art, and art now expands in exciting ways. For example, in 1969, Krueger helped design GLOWFLOW, a computer-controlled light-sound environment; an idea enlarged in 1970 in METAPLAY; and in 1971 in PSYCHIC SPACE. The floor and walls of the computerized room became, for example, the keyboard of a musical instrument, so that a person entering the room could create music by her/his movements around the room.

In the summer of 1972, Krueger was involved in taking another project, GLOWMOTION, to rural fairs in Wisconsin, giving people an entirely new kind of experience, a personalized and humanized mechanical environment. Then he worked on VIDEOPLACE (for a museum) which, he says, will take years to exhaust as an artistic and educational medium. In this computerized responsive environment it is possible to "pick up an object in New York and toss it to someone in California" in your experience. It creates scenes which can be realistic or the stuff of fantasy, with "our imagination as the only constraint."

There have already been significant experiments which show the effectiveness of such "responsive environments" in therapy. Next, in education, students will thus be given a chance to participate in the creation of art, and in teaching environments which are revolutionary in their possiblities. The schoolroom can be an enriched environment, and one in which children in one city can experience being in a classroom in another city, or in which they can visit a museum – and feel that they are actually there – without leaving their school building. The philosophical implications, Krueger says, involve a new form of human knowledge that adapts to the learner, with richer representation of problems and solutions; a greater intellectual involvement, and a way of dealing with greater complexity. The potential for theatre – and for worship in space cathedrals – is exciting as many types of media are combined in creating responsive environments.

EXERCISES AND PROJECTS

1. *Bible Study*

Read in the Gospel according to St John to study the mighty works of Jesus (= the signs or acts of God) in that part of the Gospel which Perrin and Duling, *The New Testament* (p. 349) identify as "The Book of Signs" (John 2:1–12:50). They name seven miracle stories or "signs" – changing water into wine, curing the official's son, walking on water, raising Lazarus, etc. Consider individually or in groups: What would be comparable "signs" or even "miracles" within our mission to computer science? (Computer instruments that are making it possible for the blind to see and the deaf to hear?) What is needed on the human side for these signs to happen?

Commission a science fiction writer to create a "future history" of Christian computer science *after* such a series of signs/miracles/acts-of-God have occurred.

2. *Theological Reflection*

Modern culture in all its splendor and all its glamour is now awaiting the transformation to be wrought through acts of God in the world of computers. These often occur through human efforts, events, "signs," inventions, law-making. God, of course, works through "nature" also, but if we listen for God's word and act in God's strength and creative power, our acts converge (at infinity, to speak in a mathematical image) with God's acts and mighty deeds. (See Psalm 105 for an example of the biblical record's recollection of the Lord's mighty works.)

3. *Theological Reading*

Lesslie Newbigin, *Foolishness to the Greeks* (London: SPCK, 1986). See chapters on mission to the sciences and mission to politics.

Clifford Pickover, *Computers, Patterns, Chaos and Beauty* (New York: St Martin's Press, 1990).

4. *Exercises and Discussion*

(*a*) Work out the constitution for an ideal missionary society for the execution of "mission to the world of computers." This must differentiate between computer programmers, computer ideas, computer education, etc., as in the first part of this chapter. How would such a society be affiliated to all local churches/fellowships which you know?

(*b*) Appoint a commission of scholars to study all extant science fiction, exploring images of the future *redemption* of computer science, artificial intelligence, robotics, etc. What does this imply for the church?

(*c*) A team should monitor daily newspapers such as *The New York Times* and periodical publications in the world of computers. This team can identify areas of progress and "discussion topics." Advanced computer-user groups can construct a relational data base for cross-reference among and between the items identified. Examples: developments in supercomputers, superconductors, concepts of "progress" in A.I., evaluation of software, etc.

(*d*) Discussion could focus on whether in God's sight these "news items" really constitute progress.

(*e*) For church mission agencies: How can we contribute to "mission to computers," code-named *Project Goodware* as described in the text? How can we monitor "news" of the world of computers, and distinguish "good" news from bad, theologically, in these scientific fields?

(*f*) With reference to the life of Newbigin: What kind of life is good preparation for the career culmination of being a theologian of mission (missiologist?) Who shall we appoint as church strategists for the twenty-first century? How shall we train them? What kind of missiologist is needed for planning and supervising "mission to the world of computers"?

5. *Prayers for Space-Age Missions*

Give to us, O God, brilliant young and wise old missiologists. May the young science of missiology take a leap forward in power and accuracy as it encounters the accelerating world of computer science and technology. Help us, O God, to train missioners and missionaries who can, respectively, plan to "go on mission" to space-age computer science and its emerging milieu.

Give to us, O God, guides who will introduce us to the young potential adventurers waiting for your call in their schools, colleges of engineering, academies, polytechnics. Guide the leaders of the church as they formulate and promulgate their curriculum for the training of witnesses and human servants in the world of computers.

6. *Meditation*

The power by which Christ (the power of God) reaches out to witness within and redeem the world of computer science is *the gospel* (sacrificial love). It is a living force, the center and the "archetype" of all forms of energy, the core and fount of the electromagnetic spectrum, the center of all metaphysical categories, and the origin of all true power. It is the "engine room of the universe" – both spiritual and material. It is this "good news of God," this power-to-change evil into good, which is the executive agent as we go forward in mission. It is Christ himself who educates and forms me/us as an agent of the gospel. Therefore I/we need to allow our meditations, our contemplative prayer, our worship, to be surrendered not to "God" in the abstract, but to the electrifying, rule-breaking executive power: the gospel. From now on we need to be obedient to that living power, to let it shape our lives, work, and thoughts. And it is not only power: it is good news, really good news. This is not a cliché unless we let it become one.

As we are "formed" by the gospel of love, we *become* the gospel; that is, our personalities and works or art or science or politics become conveyers of good news: which is an unlimited variety of directions and dimensions.

7. *Worship Suggestions*

Call to Worship: Use meditation above.

Bible Study on the power of the gospel and the meaning of good news.

Presentation of "good news" in the world of computer science; talk on the message of good news which we shall take to computer science.

Intercessory prayers for all who are on mission to computers or seek to witness in that world.

Sermon on the good news in relation to the world of computers.

Offertory of our willingness to seek, find, and proclaim the good news in the world of computers.

Holy Communion to consecrate what we have discovered and to take this fruit of worship out to the world in our mission to computers.

8. *Recommended Reading and Viewing*

Lesslie Newbigin's autobiography, *Unfinished Agenda* (London: SPCK, 1985). Read also his *Honest Religion for Secular Man* (London: SCM Press, 1966); his *A Faith for This One World* (London: SCM Press, 1961); and *A South India Diary* (London: SCM Press, 1951).

Film/Videos: *2001* (Clarke/Kubrick, 1968). Do we want our computers to be like "Hal 2000?" or like R2Q2 or C3PQ in *Star Wars* (George Lukas 1977). Again, does Robby the Robot in *Forbidden Planet* (1956, directed by Fred McLeod Wilcox) represent our Christian ideals? What can we learn from this about "mission to robotics"?

NOTES

1. London, SPCK 1986.
2. *Op. cit.*, 1 and chapter 4.
3. *Op. cit.*, 4.
4. *Ibid.*
5. A term promulgated by missiologist Brian Mills of England, who uses it to refer to the evangelization, through Christian mission, of any cultural institution.
6. Newbigin, *op. cit.*, (note 1 above), 10.
7. Rossman, *Computers: Bridges to the Future*, 78.

8. See the denominational computer conferences on the NWI computer network in the USA and the Christian Computer-Users Network.

9. Defined as that which produces open-ended and heuristic output, with the possibility of going beyond possible foreknowledge and sometimes the intentions of the programmers.

10. W. T. Anderson, *op. cit.*

11. Peter H. Lewis, "A Great Equalizer for the Disabled," *New York Times*, Education Life section (Nov. 6, 1988).

12. John J. Hughes (Grand Rapids: Mich.: Zondervan, 1987).

13. Produced as software by Scripture Union in Britain.

14. For example, a university ministry which assigned ministers to work with students and faculty in one discipline, or the Archdiocese of Hartford which assigned each parish to monitor and do research on a current social issue.

6

The Calling To Be
Creative and Responsible

Computer professionals may not have thought much about the idea of a "calling," that all human beings are called by God to specific works, for moral purposes, for a just social order "on earth as it is in heaven."

One way to illustrate the issues involved in the vocation of computer professionals, indeed to all in this milieu, is through the study of human nature and the "image" of Creator in the human being (theological anthropology). A second approach is through ethics, the theory of right conduct and action.

An example of "calling" is found in Jeremiah 1:4–5: "The Lord said to me. 'I chose you before I gave you life, and before you were born I selected you . . .'" It is a simple axiom of religion that God speaks to each person and calls her/him to a particular life of opportunity. Paul Tournier (1900–1986), psychoanalyst and theologian, put it this way: "God has a purpose for each of us, in every day and in every moment."[1]

In the theology of *gift* and *talent*, central to the understanding of calling, is the basic idea that each person's unique talents are given by God for "right" (righteousness and kingdom) purposes. They are not to be used for entirely selfish ends. And it is equally wrong not to use one's talents, to "bury" them, ignore them, or leave them uncultivated. The New Testament parable of The Talents (Matthew 25:14–30) makes it clear that this is irresponsible.

The Calling to be Creative and Artistic

To understand "calling" in the computer milieu, we need first to say something about the Creator. Yet what can we say about "realms of sacred Being" that is not at the same time too much and too little? This is not the place for lengthy discussion of God's being. Yet that realm of life which is God's domain is pregnant with an infinity of grace – wisdom, love, kindness, intelligence, and creativity.

Insight, glimpses into these divine/sacred realms have not only been vouchsafed to mystics; they are also part of the ordinary[2] worship of congregations, sung in hymns such as the one often sung to the tune of *Picardy* ". . . As the Light of Light descendeth, from the realms of endless day." Similarly the hymn, "Immortal, Invisible, God only wise" speaks of "Thy justice like mountains high soaring above, Thy clouds which are fountains of goodness and love."

Computer scientists, we suggest, can exercise an important part of their vocation to be creative, imaginative, and artistic by learning to "access" these sacred realms of divine being. As one accesses data through computer hardware and a software program, so one can "access" the divine realm where creativity is inspired and blossoms. Meditation, worship, prayer, and study (in dialogue with theology and the eternal wisdom of scripture) are paths to a deeper knowledge of God and our calling.

As human creativity is a partnership with God the Creator, it is interesting to note the empowerment of creative activity which is coming with new computer instruments, noted especially in the arts. It may be that God intends for all artists to become part of the computer world, and all computer designers to become artists.

The call to all people is, among other things, *to be more artistic and creative* – in partnership with the Creator. And computer tools now make it possible for amateurs to create computer art and make films. "Sunday painters" and children are now able increasingly to use "computer graphics" and other art technologies in astonishingly creative ways. We have already noted, for example, how composer-software makes it possible for even small children – with delight, and not intimidated as adults often are – to compose and play symphonies.

A rapidly growing number of professional artists and musicians express themselves primarily in computer-related media, multi-media and hypermedia, using computer-designed and empowering instruments to bring together entirely new combinations of arts and possibilities for art.

Some computer professionals are also called artists, however, because they have special gifts, for example in the design of computers or in creating artistic computer software. They, in partnership with other artists, have a calling to present exciting and inspiring new visions of our human future. In doing so, they are also called responsibly to illuminate human suffering and need; and, as all artists are called fully to express their gift, to discuss together the significance of computers in the history and future of art and aesthetics, and to uphold standards of excellence in computer art. Jenny Day, a professional software engineer, is seeking to recruit "two thousand sacred artists for the year 2000," their mission being to develop the arts of computer programming and to engage in a mission to the philosophy of art (aesthetics) itself.

Ethics: Responsibility in the World of Computers

We must next speak of ethics. It is elementary ethics that those who work in the computer world have a calling to do "right" and "good," if their conduct is to be seen as "right" or "wrong." Ethics is sometimes seen as an enquiry into the meaning of good (or *the* good), asking questions about the aim of human life. Its judgments about the chief ends of humanity are related to – or contrasted with – judgments which are scientific or artistic (aesthetic).

Ethics invites us to think about what we should do with our lives. It helps us to decide where to place our energies and actions, and how to line up our feelings with our decisions and investments. In this respect, ethics can be an integrating and healing factor in the planning of life and vocation, a clarification of values. It can release energies. It can put an end to vacillation, even to sin and crime. Ethics can help us all know where we are going, how to get there, and why we should go.

This branch of philosophy, or rather of human culture, can also help us to choose our friends and partners along the way. It is a road to God, the Supreme Good. Ethics, as a bridge from our ideas and dreams to our work, should be exciting, exhilarating, energizing, and a way to satisfy spiritual yearnings.

Before we touch upon the idea of developing codes of ethics (dynamic ethical codes) in the world of computers, it is helpful to look at some issues from the parallel perspective of moral philosophy – which is often linked to Christian ethics. So we ask: What is the *moral responsibility associated with being a computer professional?*

In a general sense, the moral responsibility of a professional, from the standpoint of the tradition of ethics, involves actively seeking the highest good, the *summum bonun*, God – known by many names. It is, as a parallel activity, to seek to make this "good" the principle, the power, and the goal of all of the dimensions of research and communications technology.

This is not just something for an individual to do: it is a matter of building computer-community which can seek and find this higher reality within which people can support each other in living up to it. We can, however be much more specific about the kind of activities which are conducive to such spiritual success in computer science and its related fields.

The key ethical words for computer functionaries, we suggest, are "compassionate," "collaborative," and "responsible."

(1) The gift and talent of being a computer professional implies a profound moral responsibility. This means a responsibility to intervene in the future development of computer science, so that it is redirected and as a result serves all of God's creatures. To make such an intervention, it may be necessary to amend one's life style. A new life style for computer professionals will be based on grace rather than mere profit, on sharing and loving rather than competing. It will turn from excessive individualism to more intentional collaborative involvement with others in responsible creation.

(2) An ethics of collaboration may involve partnership with customers. For example, entrepreneurs in the computer software business face a tremendous loss of profit from users who copy software and use it without paying for it. This theft seriously limits the mass production of that software which could reduce cost of it for all. It reduces the amount of money available for further research and new products. One solution is the continual search for new ways to prevent copying of disks, which may also limit effective use by those who legitimately purchase it.

An innovative solution has been "shareware" in which the developers and manufacturers of the software enlist their customers as partners in the enterprise. The entrepreneur sends the software out free for trial, often even encouraging copying and sharing it and inviting suggestions for improving it. On a sort of honor system it is understood that everyone who secures a copy will pay the manufacturer. Some do not pay – and there are losses in the copyright system also – but the "shareware" system is profitable. It allows for lower cost for users (sometimes it is "pay what you can"). It suggests a more compassionate and responsible way to distribute programs for Third World development.

Part of the turn away from exploitation can be an ethical decision to establish linkages between the science and art of economics and the science and art of computers. Then the "distribution of scarce goods among competing wants" can be facilitated both by the life style of computer users and by their usages of their computer networks, programs and facilities.

(3) The "compassionate computer functionary" may discover a new and appropriate life style through meditation groups of computer professionals which focus on their ethical issues and real problems; and through public worship in which they can place their lives in the larger universe of the world's need and God's perspective. Computer research and discovery can be better welcomed, recognized, and celebrated in "liturgical" settings which help computer professionals to seek out and implement a "sacramental" and "serving" quality of life. Computer music and art can open entirely new dimensions to such worship – as earlier happened with the invention of the pipe organ and cathedral.

Theological reflection on God's revelation of love and God's will for all humanity is also required. The compassionate computer functionary needs covenant groups to develop a philosophy of continuing education. There they can covenant with one another to enlarge their ethical sensitivity. They can seek a compassionate perspective to transcend the often-present conflict between technology/science and religion. Reflection upon Torrance's "scientific theology" (see our chapter 9) and its antecedents, or the history of the church's complex relationships with science, can provide a better foundation for compassionate ethics in the world of computers. Also, compassionate computer professionals might profit from the literature of futurism as an aid to study and reflection upon new and more imaginative futures for their profession.

Codes of Ethics for Computer Professionals

Ethics is a problematic and troubled field, its theories uncertain. Some philosophers[3] doubt whether a language of ethical discourse any longer exists in our culture. However, perhaps computers can be used to help improve the lot of the art/science of ethics, and assist it in becoming both collegial and cumulative.

Hitherto, ethics has been at best a "pseudo-science" in that its doctrines have not really been tested empirically in any systematic way. Its exponents or theorists have for the most part worked in isolation from one another. Ethics has been divorced from science and technology in its method and from the living God in its spirituality. Moreover, by proceeding from *individual minds*, it has deprived itself of the Christian collegial dimension of discovery and koinonia.

The impact of computer science on ethics might begin with the potentiality of hypertext and collective intelligence. For example, in law, where immediate access is now available to computerized legal case data, computers are now also being used to compare the laws of all countries and cultures to discover where universal agreements exist. This can be the beginning of a true "world law," enforceable in all courts, at least in areas where everyone agrees. Next, in the area of law, such comprehensive computer data on areas of disagreement, history of law and comparative law can provide a constructive basis for next steps and advancement in world law. (In contrast to "international law" which deals only with the relations of one nation to another.)

The same method can make a constructive contribution to ethics. The speed and "number crunching" capacity of computers can give to ethics an almost unbelievable speed of response to the actual circumstances of life. For example, the Jewish tradition is now almost completely computerized, so that the answer of traditional Hebrew values on any ethical or moral issue can be quickly and comprehensively available.

To this we add next the emerging computer tools for the empowerment of collective intelligence. Hypertext – which can make a comprehensive search through tradition in pursuit of any idea, person, or data – can make it possible, on a scale and depth never before possible, for ethicists to compare the scholarship of and work closely with scholars in all ethical and religious traditions. The whole task of ethics can take on a positive and dynamic direction. Indeed it can become the "galvanic" *search* for those principles of conduct and life, those mechanisms of technology, and those philosophies of science which will introduce, with urgency and unfailing direction, those human actions which meet the needs of the suffering and deprived.

It was Einstein who pointed out that the human race had become scientifically gigantic while remaining ethically infantile. Why is it that many computer programmers and entrepreneurs – even Christian ones – are, to be candid, ethically illiterate?

Whose responsibility is it to raise the ethical questions in the world of computers?

And whose responsibility is it to help them discover, and to publish the ethical principles necessary to honor their profession and Creator?

One answer: Computer technology is so new, so powerful, and *apparently* so distant from the traditional concerns of philosophical ethics and of moral and dogmatic theology that both the technologists and the scholars are baffled as they seek a bridge between these two unrelated worlds.

Part of the problem is that the subject of ethics has been in trouble for several hundred years. "Moral theology" has always been something of a "low man on the totem pole" in theology; and it has too often been most concerned with the formulation of totally rigid principles of right and wrong.[4] Moreover, similarly, ethics is something of an ugly sister in philosophy and has never really achieved the independent status of, for example, the "theory of knowledge" or metaphysics or logic. Furthermore, the decline of the medieval world view and the rise of humanism resulted in ethics being cut off from its divine roots and left alone in the modern world. It is no surprise that Einstein should regard the human race as ethically infantile, since responsible ethics remains a very young subject.

Ethics is sufficiently mature in its instruments of thought to make possible a more adequate code of ethics for computer scientists and professionals. However, we now live in a time when outsiders can no longer impose ethics on people such as those in the world of computers. They must develop it themselves and can use their own computer networks to get their own consciences in dialogue with those in the ethical tradition who can raise the questions that must be faced.

Codes of ethics – in the world of computers – can be maintained on line and regularly updated and revised according to the actual experience of the users. This can be done with consideration to and dialogue with the ongoing reflections of ethicists, theologians, and in response to "words of knowledge" given to the entire system by monastics or others whose speciality is to listen to what the spirit is saying to the churches and to the world.

Adequate "codes of ethics" are not simply changing, however; they exhibit growth with direction. They are neither ascending spirals nor accumulating empires of knowledge. Rather, they are designed so that they can veer with ever increasing speed towards the fulfillment of the callings of justice and service. They can help correct the finite (though huge) problems facing our society – such as the feeding of multitudes of hungry children.

In this way, the "medium" of computer science provides a possibility for ethics itself to advance methodologically as a science, and indeed to exhibit an acceleration comparable to that which is presently confined to high-tech culture. But this acceleration, in the moral realm, is "curving" in what theologians call an eschatological direction. That is, all human good will and love, energy, science, and technology are striving toward the rule of God on earth. In that striving, the cultural equivalent of "gravitational fields" bend in toward the community of peace and justice in the same way that light itself bends in the vicinity of the monumental mass of that star which is our sun.

With tongue in cheek, we suggest to computer programmers that they can create instrumentalities whereby the ethical issues (questions but not solutions) in a sentence can be flagged as effectively as a computer spell-checker flags spelling errors in a document.

More important, with a collegial search for ethical responsibility built into essential data bases and software, the ethical codes of the computer world can be ever-changing. Yet there can be a sense of direction, continually upgraded and improved, becoming friends and counselors like the laws alluded to in Psalm 119. In any case, with computer empowered collective intelligence – and even some artificial intelligence techniques – ethics can become a creative art in its own right.

Rudolf Steiner, in *The Philosophy of Freedom*,[5] speaks of the essential role of moral imagination and of the free play of ethical concepts in the mind. This free play of concepts is as much a part of the advancement of science – in the "natural" sciences, including the physical sciences – as is measurement, theory formation, and experimentation.

PROPHETS WITH A CALLING

As we reflect on ethics we consider the life of a premier *ethicist* and science fiction writer. **W. Olaf Stapledon** (1886–1950) was a philosopher and author who lived a quiet life, mainly in the Merseyside region of England. He spent some of his childhood at Port Said and was educated at the progressive school of Abbotsholme; later, at Balliol College, Oxford, he read industrial history.

His first book, *Latter-Day Psalms*, was published in 1914. For the next fifteen years little was heard of him. He was studying and inwardly preparing himself for his great work to come, marking the beginning of middle age by finishing a Ph.D. degree at Liverpool University several years before the appearance of his first full-length, non-fiction work: *A Modern Theory of Ethics* (1928).

The professionally accredited scholar then devoted himself to an extraordinarily fruitful period of full-time writing, initially in an ordinary house in a Liverpool suburb; and then for the last ten years of his life in the village of Caldy on the Wirral peninsula. He used to swim in the sea all the year round.

While raising two children with his wife Agnes, Stapledon produced his first great masterpiece, *Last and First Men* (1930). This imaginary treatise on the entire future of the human race – a science fiction exploration of ethical possibilities and issues in such fields as genetic engineering – caused a sensation on both sides of the Atlantic. In it, Stapledon explores the future biological development of species, the ethics of "Great Brains," "Vital Art" (genetic surgery on animals) and similar ventures.

Over the next few years he continued to write novels and philosophical works while preparing for his *magnum opus, Star Maker,* which appeared in 1937. It is a future history of all possible universes and the ethical issues which appear within them. Again, cast as philosophical science fiction, it is regarded by science fiction historians as the "ultimate science fiction." In *Star Maker,* a man designated by historian Sam Moskowitz as possessor of the "most titanic imagination ever to appear in science fiction," studies the philosophy of cosmology with a controlled, lucid imaginative grasp of the possible and the desirable. In this way Stapledon bequeathed to his successors a tradition and a craft in the use of science fiction for the advancement of ethics and metaphysics.

Stapledon lived for thirteen years after *Star Maker* appeared. During those years, which included the Second World War, he continued to produce science fiction, including *Sirius,* the tale of a genetically engineered intelligent supersheepdog; and *Odd John,* the story of a colony of superbright children and their fate in civilization. In 1947, he traveled to America to testify at a peace conference. His last, posthumous work, *The Opening of His Eyes,* which appeared in 1951, was a devotional tract in which he made his peace with God. He died suddenly of a cerebral hemorrhage at his Merseyside home in 1950.

One of his last works was a London lecture, given at the British Interplanetary Society in 1948, entitled "Interplanetary Man?" It remains an as-yet unsurpassed treatise on the ethical foundations of astronautics.

An International Olaf Stapledon Society was founded in 1975, and science fiction writers such as Arthur C. Clarke have acknowledged Stapledon as the noblest mind which they ever encountered. Clarke was present at Stapledon's British Interplanetary Society lecture.

What was Stapledon's contribution as an ethicist? It is, in a way, too early to tell; for we are only at the beginning of Stapledon scholarship.

Apart from his obvious work as a professional ethicist, his main contribution was perhaps to shape science fiction as an instrument for the exploration of the future . . . as a present dimension in scientific ethics. In this way, he functions as a prophet for such varied fields as cosmology, genetics, and theology, as well as literature, literary criticism, and science fiction itself.

Reading his life leads us to ask: Who will be the "science fiction ethicists" of computer science?

What sort of life would have to be led in order to arrive at a ripeness of wisdom such as possessed by Stapledon? What is the role of the study of the future possibilities of computer science in the development of ethics in relation to the world of computers, and in relation to ethics in itself?

John Sculley has told his own story in *Odyssey – Pepsi to Apple: A Journey of Adventure, Ideas, and the Future* (New York: Harper and Row, 1987). At age thirty-eight he was a highly successful young executive who had led the Pepsi-Cola Company to become number one in its industry. He had a secure future there with the potentials for increased wealth and all the comforts of life. Then one day Steve Jobs, the even younger head of the Apple Computer Company, phoned to invite him to move into the computer field. The challenge Jobs gave was irresistible: *Do you want to spend the rest of your life selling sugared water or do you want a chance to change the world?*

Sculley, as a child, had a serious speech impediment, a stammer so severe that he could hardly speak a complete sentence. Because of that he had immersed himself in the world of technology. He loved tinkering with electrical things, even at age five. By the time he was ten he was taking radios apart to convert them to intercoms and, with some friends, was building remote controlled robots with erector sets and used radio components. At eleven he became a ham radio operator. At fourteen, in 1954, he invented a cathode ray tube, using a single electron gun with three separate grids placed before the colored phosphor screen. Sculley's father took him to a patent attorney who found that another inventor, at Lawrence-Livermore Laboratories, had applied for a similar patent just a few weeks earlier. That was the patent which was the forerunner for Sony's Triniton color TV tube.

So although Sculley's business career had led him to become a soft drink executive, he had a background to interest him in the computer company. Apple was the creation of some "child wonders." Two youngsters named Steve – Jobs and Wozniak – established what became the huge Apple Computer Company in the bedroom and garage of the home of Jobs's parents. It was their dream to give computer power – up to then largely in the hands of large corporations and institutions – to ordinary people.

The way to do this, Jobs saw, was to create a powerful and reasonably priced personal computer that was easy for anyone to use. As a high school student he was bold enough to phone a major electronics company to ask for free parts and equipment for his experiments. Next, as a college dropout, he worked in 1972 at designing video games for Atari. Then at a "computer hacker's" club he met Steve Wozniak, a self-taught computer wizard who was at work on a similar dream. Jobs sold his Volkswagen van and Wozniak sold his beloved scientific calculator to raise $1300 to start their makeshift computer production line in the garage. They were successful in selling a kit for people to use to build their own computers. By 1980 their enterprise had become the second largest computer company in the world.

Jobs invited Sculley to head Apple because they needed an executive who could lead the company in imaginative new directions. Nearly everyone Sculley knew thought he was foolish to leave his highly profitable job at Pepsi Cola. However, amid these negative reactions he had one pleasant surprise. His children knew about Steve Jobs and were excited that their father was going to meet him. Sculley was enchanted when he visited Apple, finding a "creative and open environment." Nearly everyone on the staff was young, brilliant, and idealistic and "they wanted to change the world." Some were teenagers. No one worked from nine to five. The team developing the innovative MacIntosh computer worked at every waking hour. Indeed many Apple employees wore T-shirts which proclaimed: "Working ninety hours a week and loving it."

This was an entirely different world from Pepsi Cola, where Sculley, the first MBA the company employed, had started by driving a delivery truck. If Apple had put a notice in the newspaper, asking for applicants for Sculley's job, he said, it would have read: "Wanted: impresario to orchestrate a workshop of wizards." Apple was a company with fan mail from its customers, even from six-year-old children.

Selling dreams for the future turned out to be different from selling soft drinks. "Unconstrained dreaming" was required. Like science fiction writers, "we think of the crazy, totally impractical things," Sculley was told. One dreamer on the Apple staff compared the computer "as mind expander" to the turbo-charger in a car engine. "It will let people do things far beyond what they are capable of doing now." Upon this foundation, Sculley set out to create the instruments for revolutionizing and transforming education: powerful computers which children can themselves control, and which have the attention-grabbing powers of television. He wants children's learning to be a source of unending pleasure and delight.

Such tools, Sculley says, can be the basis of a twenty-first century renaissance. He sees Silicon Valley, where he now lives, to be as the city of Florence must have been in the Renaissance, the place where brilliant minds come together to make wonderful things happen. He uses the analogy of the tenth-century cathedral which took a hundred years to build. Workers spent a lifetime on it without seeing the beginning or the end of the project. Everyone in the world of computers must reach out in new directions too, undertaking a journey that will last beyond their lifetimes.

The goal is seen in a wall motto at Apple: *Now is the time for all good men and women to come to the aid of their fellow man.*

We are contributing to something that is much larger than we are, Sculley says. There is going to be a much larger intelligence on this planet and "the kids at Apple" are pioneering in that direction. He sees the world of computers as in the "slimy caterpillar stage of a metamorphosis." The caterpillar will become a magnificent butterfly: a world where "creativity permeates every facet of our work and learning."

One of his goals is the creation of a "Knowledge Navigator." Using two navigational joysticks, like an airplane pilot's controls, it will allow the user to explore the whole world of knowledge; for example to explore beauty in the details and "the depths of philosophy" comparing ideas of the present with those of ancient Greece. The Navigator will let one simultaneously grasp ideas through a mix of media alternatives, customing knowledge to suit the user. It learns too as you use it, making your exploration easy and stimulating. Such new tools, he says, are changing the way we think, work, communicate and live. They will transform the computer industry from production of hardware and software to the creation of "new facilities to think with."

Sculley thus endorses the vision of Steve Jobs, whose "beliefs and visions helped us dream of how to restore the individual's power in a society thick with institutions." We can and will "change the world one person, one computer at a time."

EXERCISES AND PROJECTS

1. *Bible Study*

Read I Peter 1:1–2.

What does it mean to be "God's chosen people"? Consider the elements of being chosen (verse 2a): (a) Chosen according to the purpose of God, (b) made a holy people, (c) by God's Spirit, (d) to obey Jesus Christ, and (e) to be purified by his sacrifice.

What does this mean for associations of computer professionals who would consecrate their work to God? And what does it mean for individual computer professionals? What other biblical texts refer to this choosing? What are the social responsibilities of this call?

2. *For Seminary/Theological-College Students*

Why/when was this epistle written? Look at I Peter 1:1. What would you say if *you* were writing an epistle today to "God's chosen people" scattered throughout the "scientific provinces" of, for example, A.I./robotics/supercomputers/computer science/technology/education/computer manufacturing and commerce, etc.? Write such a letter, in a group, as an exercise in creative spiritual writing.

3. *Theological Reflection*

If I/we are to have an adequate grasp of divine vocation, we must have an adequate grasp of what has been revealed of God. "God" denotes (refers to, describes) not only the Supreme Being, as if God is the biggest or best in a series, but the "Ground of Being." God is characterized by being (in Latin) *a se*; God has being in himself. This is his *aseity*; God's is not a contingent or derivative being; it is not one-in-a-series. God is the presupposition of all existence and of all existent creatures/beings.

However, "God" is not merely an idea; God is Reality, Ultimate Reality. In ancient terms, God is the *ens realissimus*, the most real being. All other reality, all realness, is secondary to, derivative of and dependent upon God's reality.

The idea that God and individual persons are potentially in perpetual dialog is basic to "theological anthropology," the theory of human nature which is implicit or explicit in religious and theological thought. Some basic ideas here are that a human being is composed of body, mind, soul, and spirit (sometimes the two are conflated); the soul (or higher self) is intrinsically connected to God (made of the same kind of substance), and can convey to the conscious or unconscious mind the will and the grace of God.

Sometimes the boundaries are blurred by using a word such as "psyche," which denotes both mind and soul. This ambiguity is the habitual situation of contemporary psychology and some psychiatry. For those interested in definitions and areas of intellectual demarcation, the study of the mind is the realm of psychology; of the soul, mysticism, and the spirit, is theology.

There has been a whole branch of theology, the ascetical, which has endeavored to set down the conditions under which the divine-human dialog can be facilitated.

Different denominations emphasize different ideas about "calling." Lutheran theology, for example, assigns a high place to "lay vocation," the idea that every person's work – not just that of the ordained minister of word and sacrament – is a calling.

If we are to understand – and do justice to – the "divine" side of this theological anthropology, it is necessary to have a generous interpretation of that which is denoted by the word "God." Theists – people who "believe in God" – come in many types and forms, from near-atheists at one end of the spectrum, to pantheists (God is everything) and nooists (there is nothing but God), through those who have a more or less capacious view of the nature of God.

In this respect, Christians can learn much from their eastern colleagues, perhaps particularly in the varied traditions which comprise Hinduism. We cannot here even begin to summarize Hindu theologies or metaphysics, but we can make a couple of points and suggest follow-up readings.

God is not "a being" or an infinitesimal point. The notion of supreme being as a designation of God contains a glimpse of the truth, but God is is-ness as well as being. God's being is not dependent on anything: God is not one being in a series. God's being is the matrix from which all degrees of being emanate, from which they take their being. God is uncreated: God's being is self-sufficient. Nobody "made God": God was "from everlasting to everlasting."

The world in which we apparently live – one studied by scientists – is low in moral terms. There are also higher, divine, realms of being, and God's own realms, the ones proper to the divine being, are characterized by vastness, incomprehensible range and scope and power. Our faithfulness, our self-purification, befits and equips us for citizenship in these higher realms. From them, the spiritual leaders of the human race have brought "tidings of release and redemption" – from them they have brought revelations of God's love and manifestations of God's power and grace.

The transactions between these divine realms (part of "God") and our mundane world have never ceased. And the time is coming – is now here – when the world of computer science is to be an agent in these transactions. The time has come for this divine power to be received directly into the heart and center of the computer industry.

Who shall receive this power? Who is called to be the "shaman" who transacts this sacred transfer?

4. *Theological and Ethical Readings*

William James, *The Varieties of Religious Experience* (Harmondsworth and New York: Penguin, 1982), the famous Gifford lectures,[5] provides an approach to religion through records of religious experience.

Geoffrey Wainwright, *Eucharist and Eschatology*, explains the deepest meaning of the greatest Christian sacrament, the Holy Eucharist. The same author's *Doxology: The Praise of God in Worship, Doctrine and Life* (London: Epworth Press, 1980) is an attempt to set the whole of systematic theology in the context of worship.

James Gustafson, *God and Ethics*, Part 1, *Theology and Ethics*; Part 2, *Ethics and Theology*, sketches a systematic theological basis for contemporary ethics. In *Christ and the Moral Life* (Chicago: Univ. of Chicago Press, 1979) he offers a christocentric approach to the practice of the moral life.

For an introduction to the philosophy and practice of meditation, see Paul Tournier, *The Person Reborn* (London: SCM Press and New York: Harper and Row, 1968), especially the last few chapters.

5. *Exercises*

One way to get a working grasp of the nature and attributes of God is to study chosen hymnals, exploring what is asserted (predicated) of God. What do you find there to be the properties of the divine one? Make a list, and develop from this a "working theology" of the all-holy which can then be used to construct a working "theology of calling." Hymns record the primordial religious experience of the faithful and can be a working guide to our experience of God: Who/what God is and does, etc.

6. *Specimen Prayers*

Send us friends, O God, who will lead us to you, show us the way deeper into your realms of divine being, and help us understand our calling to love and service in this way. May we not join the "fool" who says in his heart: there is no God (Psalm 53:1). Rather, may we take your existence as life's central presupposition and build accordingly. Help us by prayer so to enlarge our minds and vision that we can receive your word and revelations.

Give us, O Lord, the gift of a divine code of ethics for computer science – in each of its branches and domains – and those called to work within them. Give to us our transformed consciousness, irradiated by your power, your "commandments" in computer science that, obeying them, we may have real and eternal life.

7. *Meditations*

Meditation itself is like a magnet, whose magnetic field brings order to a previously randomized heap of (for example) iron filings. In the same way, the effort of meditation gives shape to my thought and shows me its divine pattern – its upshot.

So, I set myself to meditate on my calling in the world of computers. In this context, I thank God for my talents (as programmer or journalist or whatever) and gradually I allow that gratitude to pass over into sympathy for the human condition. I allow myself to experience God's call to be the "utmost for his highest" (Oswald Chambers), and from this thought I begin to sense a high destiny within and for the computer world.

Christopher Bryant (1903–1986) suggests that we then write down what we learn during the thoughts that follow. Those thoughts can indeed be God's word to us. (If a group meditation, what is written down might then be discussed.)

8. *Worship Suggestions*

Call to worship: For the presence of the Holy Spirit in ethics.

Bible study, Jeremiah 1 on vocation; also the recognition of Jesus of his messiahship (for example, Luke 3:21–11).

Presentation of news of those who are exercising moral leadership in the many departments of computer science.

Talk on the history of Christian ethics as it applies here.

Sermon on the responsibilities of organizations. Since this order of service can be used in industry, government, or academic settings, the basic theme should be on ethics to liberate, empower, and direct people to high purposes.

Offertory of self and ideas, intentions about computers.

Holy Communion to consecrate gifts and talents identified as part of one's calling within the world of computers.

9. *Discussion Topics*

What would be the content of a hymn written just for computer scientists? More broadly, who could compose a multi-media "rock opera" (with computer instruments) which depicts (the media being the message) the whole world of computers responding to the divine vocation of love? (Compare the rock group "The Who" and their "rock opera" *Tommy*. What might it mean for the world of computers to "praise God" with music-composing software?) See Psalm 150.

For professional and business organizations in the computer field: Do we have a systematic code of ethics for such areas of computer science as research, product development, manufacturing, marketing, sales, evaluation, staff training and recruitment, relation to wider society?

What is the theological basis of this or these code(s) of ethics for the world of computers? Where is God in it/them?

If we *don't* have such a code of ethics, can we enlist an ethicist or moral philosopher or affiliate with a theological college?

For theological colleges: What would constitute a course in the history of Christian ethics specially constructed for the world of computers?

For science fiction writers groups: What would be a future history of Christian computer ethics? Write a story or have a competition for the best story about a future gift of a new "ten commandments" for computer science.

What kind of contemporary stories (including biography) can be instructional parables?

NOTES

1. More on this, theologically, in the second section of this chapter.
2. For more illustrations, see the hymnody exercises at the end of this chapter.
3. For example, Alasdair McIntyre's *After Virtue* (London: Duckworth, 1981).
4. Note the furor, not so long ago, over "situation ethics," with its ideas that moral principles are not immutable but can only be expressed in relation to "local" circumstances.
5. London: Longmans Green, 1901 (and many subsequent editions).

7

Professional and Social Excellence in the Computer World

Everyone is in favor of excellence! Books on excellence in business are best sellers, with case studies such as John Sculley's 1987 book on his dreams for the Apple Computer Corporation.

Who in the computer world would not see him/herself as seeking excellence? Yet Ted Nelson in *Computer Lib/Dream Machines* warns of the way commercial interests have settled for the "second best," promoting machines, software, and systems that are too complicated, incompatible and mediocre. Unfortunately, Nelson says, too many people believe the advertising hype. They enter these "cloud castles" with enthusiasm that blinds them to the hands of the architects and the excitement of the salesmen. These are always promising an expensive device that will solve the problems people have with the old one.

Now too many people sit "entrapped in the dungeons of these castles," blaming themselves for lacking expertise rather than saying "*How dare they* do this to me!" Mediocrity has made something "hideously entangling and insidiously crippling," Nelson says, out of what excellence can make into something wonderfully liberating.

So those who would seek to encourage and support the computer world in a quest for excellence need to begin with a realistic and human dimension of the quest. The psychologist Abraham Maslow identified the need for excellence as fundamental to human individual and social behavior. As a consultant to major corporations, he sought to help them envisage and achieve "excellence."[1]

Maslow's work, coupled with that of Polanyi,[2] enables psychologists today to formulate a general psychological theory of excellence as native to the human mind and spirit, and as an intrinsic part of the psychology of motivation.[3] Excellence[4] is seen to be a natural desire of every human being. The pursuit of excellence – especially in work – is a fundamental socio-biological need of computer professionals, as well as people in any other kind of work.

Theologically, or in religious terms, we may say that human beings, made in God's image, have a native or intrinsic urge towards perfection (= excellence).[5] Therefore a "calling to excellence," to self-fulfillment in this context, is essential for God's people. *Psychologically*, or in secular terms, we can express the same truth by saying that we are a socio-biological species, "selected" for intellectual, emotional, and interpersonal excellence. This "interpersonal excellence" carries over into "the world of computers" as struggles against the mediocre. Human beings are biologically "rewarded" by excellence in political organization.[6]

But what *is* this excellence to which we call the computer world?

Concepts of Excellence

"Excellence" is an idea or group of ideas; it is also a concept or group of concepts. Dictionaries cannot capture the subtle range of meanings which the word serves and mediates, but we can distinguish some of its dimensions as it serves its purposes in our culture.

Literally, of course, "excellence" means that which has excelled, has outperformed another, some others, or all others in its category. In sport, excellence has to do with winning, victory, supremacy.

In business it has an overlapping meaning which is not quite so easy to pin down. It is doing better than one's competitors in output or sales, or distribution, marketing, customer service – any of the stages from product planning through sales and evaluation, paralleled by personnel management, purchasing, accounting, and so on.

In art and science, in addition to some of these ranges of meaning, there also is a more subtle quality, associated with ethical excellence. This is not so much a *comparative* quality. It has two types of meaning: "the best," to surpass competitors, including one's own best previous performance; and "the good" (God), the expression of goodness, beauty, truth, service, honor, faithfulness, compassion.

Both types of meaning of "excellence" have some value and relevance for the world of computers. Both can be employed so as to build more specific and extensive ideas of excellence for computer professionals. So here we make some suggestions intended to stimulate future thought by our readers themselves.

The concepts of excellence we specify for the world of computers are based on fundamental ethical principles, and center upon the infinite power of an outreaching compassion. So we begin with the premise that God has gifted the human race with the power of computer science so that love of neighbor and the creation of a just society can be expedited. An entirely different kind of excellence ensues, compared with one which sees computers as the handmaiden of exploitation or totalitarianism.

When computers are used for the glory of God and the healing of society, the concept of excellence presents itself as a several-dimensioned entity in which the personal spirituality of the user, the integrity of the relationships of the group of users – and the search of their commonweal – are as important as "technical proficiency" or the size or speed of the hardware or software.

Obstacles to Excellence – and Possible Remedies

We may be called to excellence, and even prone to it(!) – but what of the obstacles to excellence, since we so often fail to achieve it?

A scientist might speak of cruel, impersonal nature; a theologian of sin. Freud spoke of the price we pay for civilization and its associated excellence. It is the repression of the instincts, the development of the (often punitive) "superego" and the discontents of civilized life.

God works in history. Therefore society is the realm in which the kingdom of God is working itself out, however slow it seems to us at times. Freud, in *Civilization and its Discontents*, proposed that the "civilizing" influence of the power of love is extremely slow, and in any case is ceaselessly opposed by the forces of several death-impulses. We should not be surprised that even computers take part in what Freud called the "eternal conflict" between the two adversaries, love and death.

Norman O. Brown illustrates the theory of psychoanalysis and its role in culture (in his philosophy of history) in *Life Against Death*. He sees the whole modern period of history as contention between the forces of repression and the forces of liberation. However, his ideas have yet to be applied to the working of computers.

We would point out a reason. The "remedy" for life's resistance to excellence (goodness and bestness) is in "the spiritual life" and its practices. Let us look at just one example – prayer.

What do computers have to do with this?

If computer people are willing to dream great dreams, to rededicate their energies to goodness, to be the scientific representatives of the "have-nots," for example, there are many things they can do. They can pray in the context of their most profound and important work. Prayer is not just petition, that is, asking God for things. More importantly it is spiritual imagination, Harvey Cox says, in God's presence. It is more than a dialogue. In it we can receive – if we will – unlimited power, grace, vision, knowledge, and inspiration, even in new scientific fields. Most scientific discovery, after all, comes in the "flash of inspiration" as much or more than from lab research and experimentation.

Science itself is actually a part of God's self-revelation; and computer science – like all forms of "knowing" and knowledge – is intended by God to be governed by the go-between God, the Holy Spirit.

What kind of prayer can produce all these benefits?

It is not just "wrestling with God." It is waiting on God in contemplation or silence, computer practitioners surrendering their thoughts and skills to God. In giving themselves as computer users to God they can expect to find a radiant fulfillment of their special talents and gifts so they can take a just place in society, in science, and among the people of God of all times and races. Their calling will become visible and capable of being lived out in a spirit of service and fulfillment. Moreover, such servant living invariably is blessed with bountiful discoveries of new advances in science, ones that are more precisely geared to the spiritual progress of the entire human family.

It would not be enough of a way forward for spirituality, in the computer age, to take the contents of William James's *The Varieties of Religious Experience* and put them "on-line" (as the *Encylopedia Britannica* is computerized on line). For that record of religious experience and its meaning to become a part of science itself – Bonhoeffer's "humanity come of age" – would require cross-indexing, and hypertext where ideas "branch and jump on the screen," the computer aiding the thinker with references and implications from all areas of learning. Ideas and ways of praying that are petty and small can become as large as God's universe, just as computers have enabled such stretching of minds and energies for the exploration of outer space.

Who in the Computer World is Summoned to Excellence?

It is interesting to note the wide variety of human beings in the world of computers, to adapt the kind of classification that psychologists do to a Christian typology; and to specify how each person, summoned to excellence, must express that excellence in different kinds of activities.

Who is it, then, that is called to excellence, ethics, service, and healing? We see three categories of groups of persons who are involved in the computer world.

The first are the computer practitioners, recognized as such by society. Most people tend to think of the professionals in our world as being doctors, clergy, teachers, lawyers, etc., so let us list and reflect upon the responsibilities of

A. Students of computer science and
B. Teachers of computer science, both of whom can be
C. Inventors or
D. "Imagineers"
E. The hackers, who probe into forbidden areas
F. Engineers, including electronics engineers
G. Software designers
H. Manufacturers (employees and employers)
I. Programmers
J. Entrepreneurs
K. Media commentators
L. Analysts
M. Philosophers in the computer realm
N. Staff of professional computer associations

These computer people are called by God to "serve" society – with exellence – within a new field of science. But excellence can be empowered by the awareness of a divine vocation. It is in seeking divine power and direction that they will unlock the truth about the presence of God who dreams great dreams in and for the computer world itself.

Excellence in this calling is to consecrate their thoughts, their programs, their professional life and relationships so that their products, their communications and their aspirations are directed toward raising the whole suffering human race out of its morass of indignity and torment.

If the computer people are willing to dream great dreams, to rededicate their energies and to be the scientific representatives of the "have-nots," there are many things they can do:

(*a*) They can undertake macro-research projects beginning with poverty, hunger, disease, crime, clean water for all, and so forth, using spiritual imagination to serve the world's most fundamental needs.

(*b*) They can train their children, students and apprentices to use computers with excellence as well as in service. Excellence, we suggest, requires a kind of community which can overcome some of the individualism, isolation, and obsessive competitiveness among individuals in the world of computers. A special sense of community is needed to empower excellence not only among the types of persons listed above, but two other categories as well.

The second category of people – let's list them again to make them consciously visible in our minds and prayers – are those directly working in the church:

A. Youth workers
B. Members of congregations who work at all kinds of jobs
C. Members of intentional communities
D. Pastors
E. Bishops and Moderators
F. Archbishops and Primates, denominational executives and staff
G. Missionaries
H. Missiologists
I. Missioners
J. Evangelists
K. Monks, nuns, friars, etc.
L. The "Provincials" of Religious Orders
M. The heads (Superiors) of Religious Orders
N. Teachers in Christian schools, colleges, seminaries
O. College principals, presidents, head-teachers, etc.
P. Mission agency executives and staff in demoninations and ecumenical agencies

What is their calling in the computer world?

(*a*) First, to intercede in prayer for all those in the "computer world" and to accept some responsibility to pass on to that world what they hear the spirit saying to computer practitioners.

(*b*) Second, to use computers responsibly and experimentally so that they speak to the computer world from real involvement and experience, and not just theoretically; and so that they can use effectively the power that God, through these instruments, has made available to them.

(*c*) To develop an integrated curriculum for youngsters which uses computer art, music, data bases, and a style of learning suggested by Papert's "mind storms."

(*d*) To develop a study curriculum on "Christ and computer science" for students, laypeople in the computer world, and others who ought now to be taking the lead in reflection about using "global-scale tools" in compassionate ways.

(*e*) To reflect theologically on the history, present, and future of computer science and related technology; and perhaps as a result to develop alternative concepts, and alternative technological models which might provide a challenge and contrast to, for example, the previously discussed "media lab" at M.I.T.

> Could someone create for students and children a Christian "compassionate media lab" where technological discovery and collaboration is not only guided by the pursuit of knowledge but by compassion? A place, for example, where the earlier proposed software or robots programmed and designed to seek out and serve might be designed? In such a lab the relationships between and among the members and staff are guided not by competition but by sympathy, collaboration, worship and all the principles of "contemplative community." The monastic goals of beauty, quietude, gracious living, ceaseless prayer, and unlimited love-in-fellowship can be partnered by the ferocious appetite of science for boundless discovery and its technological consequences.

(*g*) Vocational excellence for Christian leaders in this context requires attention to many issues raised elsewhere in this work, such as devising "world heart" alternatives alongside the emerging "world brain." (This is an example of a need to expose the "cultural ideals" of the computer world view to a Christian analysis in the light of the gospel.)

To the list of people in this section we must add: theologians.

They have a urgent vocation of their own in the computer world to update the "theology of vocation" for the computer age so that the notion of "being called to excellence" and its attendant responsibilities and opportunities can be revised in accordance with the ever-growing central doctrines of God, Christ, Spirit, church, and eschaton. The doctrine of God, in particular, needs to be updated so as to combat the idea that a machine can be "God."

Social Critics

The third category in this community which must support each other for excellence is that of social critics both of religion and of computer science. Again we list them, to point up their identity and importance:

A.   Futurists
B.   Religious futurists
C.   Christian futurists
D.   Social philosophers, for example, McLuhan, Marcuse
E.   Science fiction writers who are imagining the future and often
        influencing it therefore more than they intend or realize
F.   Science fiction analysts
G.   Artists

The calling to excellence by the futurists (in computer science), for example, is to be masters of their vocation, endlessly raising their competence in the knowledge of the content of future studies. They must excel in the elucidation of the methods of futurists (forecasting, planning, Delphi method, imagining, etc.). *Religious* futurists must surrender their ideas, their products, and their professional associations and fellowship to the spirit of radical prayerful contemplation.

Christian futurism itself is a young or nascent field which can help the world of computer science to mature. Christian futurists, for example, are finding it necessary and possible to lead among the world religions that are now moving toward more effective dialogue and, hopefully, collaboration in areas of human service. One such area of collaboration can be seen in the goals of the World Conference of Religious Futurists, including the deployment of computer science for compassionate meeting of human needs as well as the advancement of professional excellence among religious futurists.

The theistic futurist is sometimes a latter-day "prophet" who sees his or her vocation not being to "justify the ways of God to man" but rather first to seek and find God, and the will of God in, for example, a scientific-technological area.

Why?

In order to lead God's people in paths of righteousness and peace – even when these paths go through (and "hand in hand" with) computers.

(*a*)   The *religious futurist* ought to be espcially qualified, if not chosen, to demonstrate to society the *spiritual* dimension of the computer world, to show the idolatrous elements of the near worship of the machine, and to expose the "ideological" dimension to thinking about reality as affected by computers.[7] Is it the God of compassion and service which is the god of society, or is the "ultimate machine" being worshipped?[8]

(*b*)   The calling of *social philosophers* in the computer world is to reflect with maximum integrity on the evolution of society and societies. These social philosophers can help the world to discern the hidden goals of social evolution. And third, they can propose new social goals which incorporate a moral redirection of computer science.

(*c*) The calling of *science fiction writers*, vis-à-vis computers, is to create what Olaf Stapledon (see preface to *Last and First Men*) called "true myth." Stapledon pointed out that science fiction should be rigorously governed by a compassionate but controlled imagination and principle of art. There are two dangers for science fiction to avoid.

On the one hand, science fiction *serves* society when it neither seeks nor extols the merely fantastic, the pornographic, or the sensational or extreme.

On the other hand, poverty of imagination *offends* against the particular "genius" to which scientific fiction writers are called. Their mission is to go boldly where no person has gone before in the world of ideas. They should explore – within realistic limitations – the direction and moral meaning of each science and technology. Their gift of vision enables them to test the limits of science itself both metaphysically and morally.[9]

(*d*) The calling of *artists* – to use art so people can see and feel, and to evaluate critically – leads to a special task for them as compassionate critics. That task is to portray more noble and beautiful alternatives for the computer world as a whole; to show desirable futures for computers-in-society in imaginative multi-media art; and to use the great gift of the artist, the gift of discernment, to depict vividly the hidden reality – and often ugliness – of evil and abusive uses of computers. For as literary critic Matthew Arnold wisely said: "Art is not as Aristotle thought, the imitation of life; it is the criticism of life."[10]

H. G. Wells in his book *Boon* satirized the eminent novelist, Henry James, accusing him of merely writing "art for art's sake," which Wells considered irrelevant if not sinful and which he contrasted with his own "art for science's sake." Theology reveals a third possibility, which can be a real help to commentators on the computer world. This might be called "art for Christ's sake" or for "God's sake."

Since art is truly the criticism of life, it is likely the search for abundant life – for all humankind. Art for Christ's sake is not functional nor is it merely aesthetic. Rather, it pours out its love and vision as it imagines and portrays the coming kingdom of God shown in loving human community and compassionate technology.

Therefore *associations* of religious computer artists-as-social-critics can help one another to earn a living while upholding so important a social task.

A call to excellence would seem to require that all persons in this world of computers come better to "know themselves," to be able to play on and use their strengths. Such an advance in self-understanding can empower them all in excellence and in service to society. We suggest that such self-knowing can be facilitated as ethical/scientific leaders – including religious futurists – use and refine our preliminary typology. "Moral Intelligence Quotients" and other kinds of self-examination can be developed for each type (group) and can be tested in practice. We would like to see "codes of ethics": for example how can Christians working in the field of "artificial intelligence" specify how "collective intelligence" (in a responsible cooperative community of scientists and others) can operate for each group-type?

We can postulate a future development in the refinement of the typologies we have listed here, as psychology – like computer science – continues to develop, to experiment and grow, to advance its scope, comprehensiveness and power. This development would be in the integration of the *depth* psychology perspective with the experimental or psychometric perspective assumed in most "differential psychology." For example, a "Jungian" perspective on the psychology of personality and differences leads to a wider outlook on the elements of human personality and its development towards "individuation." A Jungian theory of computer science, or indeed of science/technology in general, is however something which lies entirely in the future.[11]

Excellence in Practice

In this section we mentioned, and passed over, the idea of some mega-programs which call for excellence and larger vision among people in all the categories we have defined. For such mega-projects to succeed – for example adequate health care for all the world's children – there needs to be excellence in communication and collaboration between and among groups and subgroups.

An inspiring example – which suggests that more and larger mega-projects are possible – was the 1988 Sports Aid program which the London *Times*[12] called "the world's biggest event." An alleged fifty million people in one hundred twenty-eight countries around the world took part in "The Race Against Time" to raise money to fight preventable diseases – such as whooping cough which is estimated to kill fifteen million children a year. This project – and its string of events, which even included Soviet Union cosmonauts in the MIR Space Laboratory – was the brainchild of a computer company executive, Chris Long.[13] In a small way, this mega-event was a collaboration of church and computer science.[14]

This project illustrates what we mean by mega-projects, planned and coordinated by networks of computers: live television broadcasts from twenty-three cities, the "first world carnival," a four-hour long live concert from England, Spain, Malaysia, Brazil, North America and from a South Pacific island. In Britain alone, about two hundred cities and towns were involved with athletic events of all types and for all ages – even "three-legged races" and "teddy bear outings."

How might the "inhabitants" of the "world of computers" build on such a global, transnational network of compassionate persons? We want mega-projects to empower every person as a thinker, as an artist, as a servant of need; not just as a runner, not just to raise money but . . . perhaps *science on the run?* They can undertake macro-research projects beginning with poverty, hunger, disease, crime, clean water for all, and so forth.

The Future of Excellence

Much of the cheap commercialism that has replaced excellence in business, and of the bandaid improvisation that is involved in mediocre compassionateless politics, is the result of a loss of the religious sense of calling. To enquire into the future of excellence leads to the future of revelation, or religion, or the future weave of science/religion.

To enquire into the future of excellence is also to enquire into the future of evil. This book lacks the space for a theological discussion of evil or for a detailed account of the need for religious futurists to ask about the circumstances under which God's presence can be more visible in the world.[15]

We can, however, say this much: The Christian gospel is concerned with the defeat of evil, including the terrible evil manifest in the unnecessary suffering of so many millions of the world's children. Therefore, anything contributes to the growth of excellence if it invites the goodness of God into the world – including the "world of computers" – so that God's kingdom motivates a larger proportion of human life and affairs and contributes to the growth of excellence.

What seems to be at stake here is what could be called "the healing of the world's psyche." The major question about evil, we suggest, is not so much *why* there is evil, but *where* it is, so that it can be a target for redemptive, transformational activities. It may seem strange, but to philosophize about evil seems often to abet it. Computers, we suggest, can greatly help in mapping – as never before possible – the activities of evil, death-dealing forces, whether they are political despotism, organized drug crime, famine or abject poverty, or hurricanes. Also, computers can be used to map, interconnect, and mobilize the forces of goodness to act in the face of evil.

In the last analysis, however, it is God alone who is the sovereign enemy of evil and who is the guarantor of its defeat. The excellence needed for people in key vocations to become adequate partners in coping with and transforming evil comes with the Spirit and power of God. Therefore, our last two chapters are devoted not so much to computers alone, but to the future of humanity's many-layered encounters with God. So we let the Bible have the last word on excellence:

"Who has determined the course of history? I, the Lord, was there at the beginning, and I, the Lord, will be there at the end . . . the Lord says, 'Do not cling to events of the past or dwell on what happened long ago. *Watch for the new thing I am going to do. It is happening already – you can see it now.*'" (Isaiah 41:4 and 43:18–19)

PROPHETS OF EXCELLENCE

Matthew Arnold (1822–1888), the mid-Victorian author, was a literary critic (and, more generally, a critic of culture), a poet, and inspector of schools. He is probably best known around the classrooms of the world for a single poem, "Dover Beach." He was also notable for his lifelong quest to discriminate between the *really* excellent (good) and the *apparently* excellent. Here is his relevance for this chapter. He seems to have practiced what he preached, for he is remembered as one "who loved to find the best in everyone" (Frank Harris).

It was in various books of essays that Arnold developed his aesthetic or theory of art. *Literature and Dogma* (1873) is the most important of his writings on religion. *Culture and Anarchy* (1869) is his chief work in social criticism.

During the mid-Victorian era he became a kind of one-man conscience of the English-speaking peoples. He accomplished this by his determination to establish standards of true excellence which would apply to art, religion, culture, history, and even perhaps science. He developed his concept of the "good" in his essays and exemplified it in his own poetry. Arnold knew that "excellence is not common and abundant" (his essay on Milton).

Arnold was son of Thomas Arnold, famous clergyman-headmaster of Rugby School, who helped change the face of English education. His father gave his children a home in which prayer, criticism, education, and an abundance of love were happily intermingled.

Most of Arnold's poetry was written before he was thirty-three and practically all of it before he was forty-five. It was, perhaps, not his most significant contribution to society. *Prose* was to be the chief literary instrument of his maturity. From the time of his 1857 election to the chair of poetry at Oxford University (age thirty-five) he began to write it regularly. His subsequent work included strictly literary criticism, such as his first published lecture series *On Translating Homer* (1861), and a wider philosophy of the role of critical evaluation in culture. For example, in *Essays in Criticism* (1865), he describes the damage which can be done to a nation by the lack of any widespread belief in the validity of standards of criticism. Such a lack will lead the intellectual life of society to run easily into "haphazard, crudeness, provincialism, eccentricity, violence, blundering."

Here we touch upon his notions of excellence. Criticism can help to reinvigorate our intellectual life and can serve future creative writers by discharging its true function. This is "simply to know the best that is known and thought in the world, and by in its turn making this known, to create a current of true and fresh ides." Doing this, it will contribute to the production in time of an intellectual and spiritual situation of which creative genius will be able profitably to avail itself.

It is an important part of Arnold's concept of excellence and its nourishment in society that criticism is to be directed not only upon works of art but also upon life in general! He believed that the habit of dispassionate appraisal fostered by strictly literary criticism can be of the widest social usefulness.

Arnold's concept of criticism (whether of life or art) shows him to be very close to what Bertrand Russell later called "The Scientific Outlook." For Arnold, criticism must be essentially the exercise of a freely ranging, open-minded curiosity. It must be disinterested, refusing to lend itself to ulterior (such as political) considerations.

Matthew Arnold, the great "man of letters," shows us a life admirable in its sincerity, its intelligence, and its pursuit of a truly wise society. In his prose, he gives us a model of the value to the community of flexible, non-specialist critical intelligence. Writing on religion, politics, education, and literature, he helps us dare to exercise a free play of the critical and generous spirit of intelligence upon our lives and our cultural products. We are told of him ". . . his nimble intuitive intelligence, his urbane wit, and his preeminent sanity make him one of the most stimulating and engaging of our commentators upon literature and upon life."[16]

Who will be the Matthew Arnold of the "world of computers" – carrying forward not only his concept of criticism and excellence, but developing them so as to promote cultural excellence in the world of computers?

Seymour Papert is unique in his quest for excellence in education, in that he is both a computer specialist at Massachusetts Institute of Technology, and for a while at the World Computer Center in Paris; who also is an expert in child development and psychology, having worked in Switzerland with Piaget. His book *Mind Storms: Children, Computers, and Powerful Ideas* presents a restless challenge to the entire educational establishment. He laments the fact that most people use computers only for games, entertainment or business, overlooking the fact that computers can bring excellence into the way people think and learn.

He scolds teachers, textbooks, computer software publishers, and all the experts in traditional education for expecting so little of children and for using computers simply to reproduce outmoded, bankrupt styles of teaching. He shows how to use computers to open the minds of children to much more powerful, exciting, and effective ways to learn.

Papert designed a computer language, especially for children, called LOGO. While he is an excellent theorist, he also conducts practical demonstrations, especially using as a laboratory a primary school where every child has a computer.

One view of excellence, in education and learning, is "holistic," seeking to break down the lines between different sciences and disciplines and the barriers that have separated physical sciences from knowledge of the self. "Only rarely," Papert says, "does some exceptional event lead people to reorganize their intellectual self-image in such a way as to open up new perspectives . . ." He shows how excellence in the use of computers – compared to mediocre uses in most schools – can help learners free themselves from methods that have spiritually and intellectually crippled pupils in the past.

LOGO is a computer language for children to use to learn math and science – and indeed all learning – in the same natural way in which they learned to speak their mother tongue. Children who use Papert's computers and programs are not "taught" the laws of nature, for example, but are helped to discover them for themselves. Very young children learn truths they cannot yet put into words.

Excellence in education, he shows, involves a kind of adventure, in opposition to traditional drill and rote learning. His research has demonstrated that children, when they take control of the computer and direct their own learning, can then "establish intimate contact with some of the deepest ideas . . . from the art of intellectual model building."

When very young children use a computer programmed in LOGO, they can command a "turtle," a device for drawing, so as to create for themselves a continually challenging and expanding learning environment. This excites small children with the discovery that – instead of being intimidated by the computer – they can take control of it and manage this sophisticated technology. They can use it to solve problems, to learn by doing, and to discover their own ways of learning and thinking.

This, Papert shows, is excellence in education and in all of life.

EXERCISES AND PROJECTS

1. *Bible Study*

Read Matthew 5:48. "Be ye therefore perfect, even as your Father in heaven is perfect." What does this call mean for the world of computers?
Consider:

(*a*) The philosophy of science being used – the ideas and ideals of scientific method – the understanding of science.

(*b*) The philosophy/theology of technology at work: What is the element of compassion present within it? What is your/our understanding of perfection in technology? (For theology students: What is your christology of technology?)

(*c*) What is "perfection" in communication among and between computer users?

d) What is "perfection" in education for the use of computers?

2. *Theological Reflection*

Excellence in its supreme form belongs to God; in God it is intrinsic or natural: it is of God's nature. Human life is characterized by imperfection, and though we fitfully strive for excellence, we also strive to avoid it in our laziness. This is the tragedy of our nature, governed as it is by what some theologians think of as the "fall." The theologian Emil Brunner speaks of "man in revolt" in his book with that title.

St Paul knew this twin-mindedness of human nature. "The good that I would do, I do not . . ." he writes to the Romans (Romans 7:14–25). He finds the remedy in Christ. "Who will rescue me from this body that is taking me to death? Thanks be to God, who does this through our Lord Jesus Christ" (Rom. 7–24–25, *Good News Bible*).

Christians believe, then, that it is God whom we must seek if we are to attain deliverance and its consequences for excellence. God (Christ) comes to us through the Holy Spirit – in the church and its councils, services and sacraments, in the quietude of prayer, in the fellowship of groups and Christian friends, in the study of the Bible.

So, then, we need to build Christian community if we are to have any hope of sustained excellence in our place in the world of computers. "Two or three together" invoke the additional companionship of Christ, so we should ask how much we are seeking him *in the context of our work with computers*.

3. *Theological Reading*

To develop the theme that "excellence" is still coming into the world and that God is helping a better future come into being, see:

Jurgan Moltmann, *Theology of Hope* (London: SCM Press, and New York: Harper & Row, 1967).

Alfred North Whitehead, *Religion in the Making. Science in the Modern World*.

For theological students, see the periodical, *Process Theology*.

For a wider review of relevant theologies, see William Nicholls, *Systematic and Philosophical Theology*. The Pelican Guide to Modern Theology, vol. 1 (Harmondsworth and New York: Penguin, 1969).

4. *Exercises and Discussion*

(*a*) Groups of students, church groups, etc.: Identify *examples* of "excellence" in computer journalism, education, technology, industry, planning, and in application to human need.

(*b*) Children's groups, Sunday school, etc.: Have children tell stories or draw pictures, or otherwise describe what they think of as excellence in fields like television/video, electronic toys, etc. This can be completed by helping them design or invent their own toys . . . thus teaching them that not just religious but also scientific excellence is also under the guidance of the Holy Spirit.

(*c*) For general discussion: What is the relationship between *holiness* and *excellence*? Discuss with reference to the Ten Commandments.

(*d*) What is excellence in terms of social responsibility? Compare Amos 5:21–24 with the parable of the Good Samaritan (Luke 10:25–37).

(*e*) With reference to Luke 10:29 ("Who is my neighbor?") discuss: Do computers (that is computer networking) help us to know who our neighbor is and – through "eye-in-the-sky" satellites and other technology – where the neighbor is and what he/she needs?

(*f*) If we are "our brother's keeper" (Genesis 4:9), and all nations (Matthew 28:19) are our brothers and sisters, how can excellence in computer science/technology help us to reach out to those sisters and brothers in all lands? What needs to happen if such excellence is to become a reality?

(*g*) Questions for organizations, for example Christian computer-users groups, computer businesses, churches, denominational offices, computer education/teachers' associations, computer employment agencies, information technology journalists, associations of science fiction writers, etc.:

How do we study concepts of excellence in our organization? What are outstanding examples of excellence in our area?

How do our goals for the next two to five years reflect a commitment to excellence?

What do we understand to be moral excellence within organizations?

Which organizational theorists have impressed us most? What are their ideas of excellence?

How do the group dynamics within our organization and its satellites or franchises show excellence in group processes themselves?

5. *Specimen Prayers*

(*a*) Give us, O God, a pathway to meditation suited to our time – so that, seeking you as the Spirit and core of all true excellence, we can find you, and, finding you, uphold true greatness in our world.

(*b*) Show us, Lord, the things we need to inject in our lives and thoughts, so that, ridding ourselves of slovenliness, we may find you, the Spirit of perfection, as the shining center of what remains.

(*c*) Send us, Lord, friends and lovers who will bring to us such depth of inner healing that we may leave all secondary pleasures and freely choose you, the perfect, as the one in whom we shall henceforward invest our energies and the one in whom we shall rest our thoughts.

(*d*) Give us, O Holy Spirit, patterns of worship suited to the space age, and suited to the world of information technology. Help us progressively to refine our grasp of the philosophy, the theology and the practice of worship, so that in our services of worship henceforward we experience your healing power and leadership in ways suited to the discovery of excellence in the world of science/technology (computers, genetics, biotechnology, space travel, etc.)

6. *Meditations*

Excellence is the spiritual core and centre of the cosmos. It is its true meaning, its origin, its high destiny. Moral excellence, ethical excellence, excellence in art and beauty, truth and love – these are the cluster of qualities of deity which inhere in our universe; for this world, this cosmos is God's.

The spiritual life is that which makes this hidden or latent excellence, this glory, move into open manifestation. In Christ the final glorious consummation of the universe has begun; we live in the end-times.

The activities of the spiritual life, rising to a climax in acts of charity and prayer, of worship and meditation, are those which dig in the divine gold mine of limitless excellence and return with new treasures of knowledge, love, character, and power.

May we then, by God's grace, implant the habits of the divine life of excellence, the practices of the spiritual life, at the core of the practices of the world of computers and its associated technology.

7. *Worship Suggestions*

Call to worship: Use meditation above.

Bible study on perfection: Deuteronomy 32:4, expounded with reference to the perfection of the Lord; perhaps a careful exegesis of the whole of Psalm 52; followed by Paul's letter to the Romans, chapters 7 or 8, St Matthew on perfection, 5:48.

Presentation of news of examples of moral or scientific or religious excellence in computer science.

Talk on the theology of excellence in computer science.

Recollection of God's actions in history (for example, Psalm 78).

Sermon on the way in which Christ gives us access to the divine excellence and holiness.

Offertory of our concepts of excellence and our plans/hopes for excellence in the world of computers.

Holy Communion to consecrate lives dedicated to the advancement of excellence in our work, especially in the world of computers.

8. *Further Reading*

On the human need/capacity for excellence: Abraham Maslow, *The Farther Reaches of Human Nature* (Harmondsworth: Penguin Books, 1970).

On the concept of excellence in corporations: See John Gardner, *Excellence* (New York: Norton, 1984).

On excellence in education, see: Seymour Papert, *Mindstorms: Children, Computers, and Powerful Ideas* (New York: Basic Books, 1980).

On excellence in cultures see Boris Ford, ed., *The Pelican Guide to English Literature* (Harmondsworth: Penguin Books, 1969); and Kenneth Alcott, ed., *The Poems of Matthew Arnold* (London: Longmans, 1965).

NOTES

1. Some of Maslow's helpful papers on this subject are in his book *The Farther Reaches of Human Nature*. His pioneering work *Psychology of Science: A Renaissance* has some overlapping material of equal importance as he surveys the quest of scientists for excellence.

2. See our chapter 1.

3. Those who wish to study this further can consult Cofer and Appley's classic treatise *Motivation: Theory and Practice*.

4. According to human potential, humanistic or third force psychologists, terms explained at the beginning of Maslow's *Farther Reachers of Human Nature* (Harmondsworth and New York: Penguin Books, 1970).

5. This was our theme in chapter 6.

6. Those interested in taking this theme further can study the formidable treatise, *Sociobiology*, by Edward O. Wilson. A theological counterposition to this is the recent work of Arthur Peacocke, *God and the New Biology*.

7. See Myron Kruger, *Artificial Reality*.

8. See the book of that name by Pamela McCorduck.

9. Community of St Polycarp.

10. See "2000 sacred artists paper" privately circulated by Jenny Day.

11. There is plenty of work for future psychologists! For further reading, see Andrew Samuels, *Jung and the post-Jungians*, and on the Jungian approach to individual differences, see Myers and Briggs, *Gifts Differing*. The Jungian-based

personality test, the Myers–Briggs Personality Inventory, is now quite routinely used to help clergy to more fully develop in personality.

12.   See David Sapsted, Peter Davenport, and Patrick O'Hanlon, "50m in the world's biggest event," *The Times* (September 12, 1988).

13. Of the money raised in developed countries, twenty per cent was retained to help indigenous youngsters, while the remainder went to international organizations. Poorer nations kept all the cash they could raise.

14. Pope John Paul II, then touring Zimbabwe, gave a public blessing to the efforts of fifty million participants.

15. We suggest that the core task of religious futurists is to facilitate the coming of *Divine Life on Earth*, which is the title of a book by the Hindu mystic, Sri Aurobindo.

16. J. D. Jump in the chapter "Matthew Arnold," in Boris Ford, ed., *The Pelican Guide to English Literature*, vol. 6, ("From Dickens to Hardy," 1969 revised edition), 323.

8

What is God Doing
in the Information Age?

Alan Kay has been described as one of those theoreticians whose ideas are shaping the emerging information age. He has done much to achieve his vision of the computer as a powerful instrument *for all people*, universally available, rather than a tool controlled by an authoritarian bureaucracy.[1] Kay has especially wanted to empower children so that ordinary youngsters can not only use exciting computer instruments to learn – to prepare them for a rapidly changing society – but so that they can program computers to do any creative thing they wish.

Kay considers much of his own schooling to have been a waste of time. He was very intelligent and schools filled his mind with facts but did not teach him how to think. By contrast, in a racially diverse school which is a laboratory for experimenting with Kay's instruments and ideas, the pupils are so delighted and get so absorbed in their work that the teachers have to beg them to go home when the dismissal bell rings. Kay gives the children a computerized environment to explore and a style of learning which "takes big adult questions and recasts them as children's questions." Children, he says, take an artistic approach to such creative activity.

This is one illustration of many remarkable things that are happening at this moment of human history; at this "turn of the ages," to use the language of Klaus Koch, a theologian who specializes in the prophets of Israel. In Isaiah 43:16–21 as translated by Koch, we read:

Remember no longer the events of the first time (*risonot*), no longer consider the things of primordial days!
Behold! I am doing a new thing (*hadasa*)
It is already springing forth, do you not perceive it?
This time I am making in the wilderness a way (*derek*) . . .

It is said of Alan Kay that he speaks of today's technology as if considering the artifacts of a backward civilization. The present time hardly interests the prophet Isaiah, Koch says. His emphasis is on a new kind of time, a new *derek* which will far exceed the analogies of the early time. He emphasizes positive active powers which move from God to humanity so as to evoke the maturing of history.

In his discussion of Ezekiel, Koch points out that the prophets were not much interested in metaphysical questions. They were concerned with "metahistorical reflection" about the reasons for the evil prevailing in the wilderness of the present moment. Who, they ask, is responsible for the shattered conditions in the home country, and for the misery of men and women who are refugees?

They asked the same question we are asking: what is God doing? What is God asking scientists to do at this hinge-point in history?

Koch says that "God's creation is still in a process of becoming." The prophets, Koch says, assume revolutionary change, after which history will continue to run its course in a new environment "with new anthropological, sociological and mythical conditions."

We ask also: What might be the "positive active power" which God is sending into the computer world in this information age? What is God revealing of himself? Professor A. D. Ritchie[2] has pointed out that ". . . history cannot be written without a philosophy of history." So we ask these questions within the framework of a philosophy which sees history as the working out of God's creative and redemptive endeavors.

Anything we say about God's action in the world of computers, about what God is doing in the information age, must be offered tentatively, for purposes of discussion. Perhaps we can take some clues from the illustrious Karl Rahner who only published "remarks," mainly in the form of "theological investigations" rather than seeking to propose systematic theological answers.

David Lochhead, a Canadian theologian who has used computers extensively in biblical and theological research, has offered some tentative beginnings for a theology of computers at conferences of the Church Computer Users Association.[3] In the same spirit we offer some early thoughts, resulting from our theological reflections on what God is doing, and regard what we say here as little more than crude sketches of a new and vast continent of needed theological research. It will have to be filled in by future explorers and their partners, the map makers. A theology for the computer/information age, we suggest, will ask if God is not doing at least the following things:

God is Revealing More of Himself

Human beings, especially in the work of computer-empowered scientists, are learning more and more about creation; for example, in astronomy and DNA research and how to become actively involved in shaping the future of evolution.[4] Let us look at some possiblities.

That God is revealing more of himself as we see the distant stars more clearly can be a shocking notion for those who think that the only and final self-revelation of God took place in New Testament times. Suppose, though, that God is in fact revealing more of himself. What might it be? God's power, urgency, intelligence?

Could it be that the doctrine of the Holy Trinity, with its concepts of the internal relationship of the persons of that Trinity, is not in fact the last word to human beings about God's being in himself; and that "hyperwebs" (the interrelated and interactive connections between all knowledge and clusters of computer people who use them) may reveal God's even greater complexity and love?

Thus, it may be that at this juncture of human history the Creator is revealing – in part through computer science – more of his own high and hitherto unknown intrinsic inner relationships. God may be showing his presence in the infinitesimal, the microscopic as much as the macrocosmic or cosmological; and what applies to supercomputers and artificial intelligence will also apply to room-temperature superconductors and the promised limitless free energy predicted of clean nuclear fusion techniques.

Because God is revealing more of himself, God may be shattering and expanding our primitive ideas of revelation. If God is thus revealing his power in the context of technology, God may be forging a "new covenant" in which *henceforward science and technology* (transcending religion/science dichotomies) *can be the context of both faith and the sacred*.[5]

Any revealing by God of more of divine intelligence in the phenomena of "smart computers and robots," for example, suggests that the teachings of the church may need to be updated to include divine intelligence (and creativity) as well as divine love among his cardinal attributes. Thus a doctrine of divine "collective intelligence" might be added to the teaching about the Holy Spirit, with its revelation of the internal economy of God. To those who protest that it would be presumptuous to "add to the dogmas of the church," we reply that it would also be presumptuous, if not foolish, to maintain that God is not living and active, that theology is the only science whose subject matter is finite and whose context is fixed!

Is Christian truth limited to what uneducated, unscientific people of a more primitive time could understand?

If God is revealing more of his own "superintelligence" (a concept whose properties are hardly yet probed or mapped), God may be healing the split between heart and head. Thanks to computers a more adequate "theology of intelligence" may be on the horizon.

The concept of intelligence itself has an interesting history. In the early post-medieval period it was a concept which referred to information – a commodity or intellectual substance. With the appearance of experimental psychology, at the turn of the last century, it came to mean a dynamic activity, a *processing* of information. Piaget and Inhelder endeavored to give a genetic and philosophical basis to the concept and distribution of "intelligence."[6] And it is now seen that individuals have at least seven kinds of intelligence, including artistic, abilities of "the heart," abilities to empathize with others, for example. Now with the current research into "artificial intelligence," and computerized "encyclopedic intelligence"[7] we can juxtapose the doctrine of the Holy Trinity with the ecclesiastical emergence of "collective intelligence." Then we begin to have something worth saying about the infinite complexity of the intelligence of God which is now revealing itself more powerfully in the world.

Might it be that computers are part of a continuing revealing by God of the complexity that is involved in the universe, and which therefore increasingly is brought into the awareness of the human community by post-modern science? Is God not involved in the mind-stretching tools that can help human beings understand his creation, that may help give responsible and compassionate answers to the questions being raised by astronomy, physics, biology, etc.?

Is God Continually Opening the Way to a New Theology?

Christian theologies have come and gone across the centuries because they have been efforts to understand God in light of the best current thought in philosophy; and there has not yet been an "information age" theology because it must take into account much more of what science is learning about God's universe *than has ever before been possible.*

If a space information kind of theology is actually coming – some like David Lochhead are calling it "digital theology" and Kirby is calling it "vector theology" – then it will on one hand be the result of the shattering of the old. In the coming of a new age – as has been true in the past – God is acting as the great iconoclast, shattering the idols of existing religiosity, cheap piety, and outmoded ideas – as the classical prophets of the Old Testament shattered the "religiosity" of ancient Israel and declared its cultic religion bankrupt. In Amos 5:21 (Good News Bible translation), the Lord says: "I hate your religious festivals, I cannot stand them."

One theologian has said, scornfully, that computers have no more to contribute to theology than typewriters. This suggests that he has not paid much attention to, for example, the CYC project initiated in 1985 by a consortium of American computer companies to begin the process of encoding and representing all the world's knowledge in an interactive system: empirical facts, beliefs, heuristics, methods for navigating through the whole system of human knowledge, and more. The aim is to make it possible not only to search through all of human knowledge and tradition, to make connections, to discover what is known and where research is needed, but to help each user classify, abstract, and analogize expert knowledge and broad or common sense knowledge.

Intelligence is being redefined, Harmon says,[8] not only as "something dependent on numerous pillars of expertise backed by general knowledge and analogical reasoning; but is also expected to transcend encapsulated human intelligence and the severely restricted frontiers of human knowledge." Such "supra-intelligence," he says, may grow and develop as "pluralistic intelligence distributed in networks, integrated circuity, institutions and even as a component of . . . eugenic efforts." Such research is based on the expanding scope of knowledge about the human brain and intelligence. And Glynn Harmon asks *what world views should govern the organization of all knowledge?*

If, in the information age, God is linking theology to a philosophy of science, and to vast amounts of scientific information, then in the case of epistemology or "the theory of knowledge," computers may actually enable (and cause) the theory of knowledge to be linked with the theology of redemption. We suggest this because the capacity of supercomputers enables the human family to gather, store, process, and distribute "sacred information" – about the suffering of the poor, for example – along with all other coordinated information. A Christian "theory of knowledge" has as much or more to do with serving Christ's "least of these" (Matthew 25:31–44) as with abstract ideas about deity.

If, indeed, the Lord through the explosion of scientific knowledge has been shattering the mould of theology – which increasingly is done in "bits and pieces" rather than as a systematic whole – then a new theology may bring with it a new shape to religion also; a recasting and enlarging of the intelligence and compassion of Christianity and indeed of all the world's religions.[9] More will be said about this in chapter 9.

We suggest here, however, that this more loving (Christlike) and scientifically rooted Christianity may find itself with an enlarged understanding of the "attributes of God." If we follow tradition in "listing" such attributes, are we entitled to assume that the list or its organization is exhaustively known and entirely complete? If not, is it possible that either other attributes of God are revealing themselves (by his grace) in computer science; or perhaps more likely, that computers will help us to know something more about the relationship between and among the revealed attributes of God? For example, God is not only gracious, but powerful. The power of science is vividly seen in supercomputers as used in NASA, for instance. So maybe God is revealing to us more of the inner structure, scope, and meaning of power itself.

Perhaps most important – especially in taking account of the needy and helpless of the world – God through a new theology may make possible a quantum leap in forwarding his mission. Computers are making mission possible on a scale so vastly enlarged from anything that has gone before that it is truly a qualitative and not a quantitative change. The sum of this advance in speed, in scope and in power in many simultaneous dimensions can enable mission planners to plan "macro research projects." They can also plan more macro action projects of a higher order and dimension of magnitude than all that have gone on before in the Christian era. Thus younger mission thinkers can begin to think of "hyper mission" and ultra mission (such as mobilizing to save the ecology of the planet). Such a new vocabulary, parallel to the powerful new technology which is available, can help us enlarge our imagination and understanding of a new era of global love and justice.

God is Creating a New Era and Community of World Love

Could it be that God, according to his own high purposes, is now equipping the church with the tools to complete the proclamation of the gospel, so that the entire human family – to use the language of Buckminster Fuller – "can graduate and ascend to a higher sphere" of love and justice? Maybe, some "prophets" suggest, God is giving a *new direction* to history. Perhaps, instead of equipping humanity with technology to "escape" from planet earth, leaving it as a "ghetto," computers are equipping us to turn inward for a while to get the human house in order first. Only then will humans be entitled to turn our attention to the galaxies and beyond. This "new direction" would be the species counterpart of the repentance to which Jesus summoned individual persons.

In the H. G. Wells 1937 movie "Things to Come," the direction of human history is inexorably astronomical: in glowing terms, actor Raymond Massey summons humankind to take its place among the stars. If, however, such "graduation from earth" is accomplished on the backs of the poor and at their expense, it can only be described by that cruel simple biblical word: sin. Or, scientifically and socio-biologically, it is counter-productive in terms of macro evolution.

The idea of "collective intelligence" empowered by computers, suggests that the new human direction revealed by God is not towards Alpha Centauri, for example, but is toward *one another*, first perhaps toward misery and suffering such as in Bangladesh, Soweto, or the Bronx. The stars come later, when we are ready, when the human race has grown up to more responsible maturity and community. Humanity should not behave like a teenager who wants to use dad's car before being mature enough to do so responsibly.[10]

This means an extension of love and compassion, reaching to the far ends of the earth. That is now more possible than ever before through the power of supercomputers and related communications and research technology. The technology now exists such that "all may be saved" from hunger and degradation.

The human vocation is being revealed as love. Moreover, the allegedly rapidly coming time – when artificial intelligence may surpass the intellectual performance of any one human being, even the most brilliant – could be seen as God's gentle reminder to the human race that its vocation is neither mechanical nor intellectual alone, but *is love, truth, goodness, beauty, courage – in other words, spiritual community*.

So the question is not whether computers or robots will ever outthink us, but whether they will ever be more loving than we can be!

In the same way that the term *homo sapiens* was adopted as a result of a scientist's vision of human identity, so the hegemony of computers can lead to a deeper insight into human identity: we are not just "sapient" (with its emphasis on knowledge and thinking) but "agapens": our business is agape-love of neighbor, ourselves, and God.

The consolidation of this insight would indeed be a "new thing": a new theology, a new name, a new identity followed by a new destiny.

God is Creating a World Community of Justice

On the basis of Deutero-Isaiah and Ezekiel, who show God "doing a new thing," we suggest that the "new thing" God is doing in the information age is an extension of justice as never before. We already see how injustice can be exposed by the electronic media. Next now, the information age comes into being as a world/human community, all people linked together via human/technological networks. As we are told that in God's sight "every hair on our head is counted" (Matthew 10:30), so the needs of every child among our six billion planetary citizens can now be known, kept track of, and served by high technology governed by divine/human love.

Thus the information age can inaugurate a new era of universal justice. Not only can the bodies of hitherto overlooked or forgotten children be adequately nourished and cared for; but also their minds/psyches can be truly nourished. We know how much a child depends upon early experiences of love if she/he is to thrive and learn and grow.[11] We see God at work in computer networks and data bases (such as PeaceNet) which demonstrate new power for justice-serving organizations.

God now brings these together in the creation of a new concept of the "people of God." Justice and love require a supportive community, which brings us back to the notion of a "new covenant" and more. Is God giving us an enlarged view of what it means to be God's people? The gift of high and hyper technology forces theology to revise and expand its understanding of the children of God to be the entire global community, and to clarify how the theology of the "people of God" deals not only with privileges but with greater responsibilities.

In the info/biological/space age, our responsibilities must center around scientific training as well as religious commitment. This requires a *concept of world citizenship* in which God calls scientifically-minded world citizens to express their religious values by caring equally for the environment and for all the world's children.

Thus the "new thing" just may be the revelation of the possibility of computer-network-related, sacred-scientific communities all around the world, the totality of which can constitute a spearhead in moral and technological evolution or the progress of the human race.

Part of this understanding of the "people of God" is a better view of "human nature" which may be coming, in part, through computer science and robotics research and technology. Theologians speak of "theological anthropology" or the doctrine of humanity. The psalmist asked: "What is man that thou art mindful of him?" When scientists describe computers as a new stage in human evolution, and when genetic engineering and cyborg planning become a cultural imperative, theologians can ask whether God is revealing new potentialities and duties in human nature itself.

Can we assume that everything that could be known about human nature is known? That would trap theology in a static view of human nature. A larger theological view of human nature might provide, for example, a basis for more adequate dialogue with and contribution to the planning of robotic science and genetic engineering.

Might it be that God is calling the people of God to show the way forward in genetic engineering, for the scientific and moral development of human beings in both our biological form and "species activity"? Until theologians can show the divine meaning of the potential gift of genetic engineering, their leadership will continue to pass over to those who may have no specifically moral or ethical training or commitment.

So a new and enlarged concept of the "people of God" may take form, in part, through a collective knowledge which integrates them into a "thinking/scientifically oriented community" which can better engage and use all truth that scientists discover. In speaking of such a corporate "brain," Ernest Breton[12] sees the goal as enhancing individual thinking within the context of the whole, not regimenting it. Thus the "learned knowledge of the whole" could be mobilized to deal with problems.

A religious organization or a community can thus become a powerful kind of force by bringing together the computerized "knowledge bases" of each individual and group. Such a combination of brains and experience can "come alive" as a corporate brain as each routinely adds knowledge and experience in using the common knowledge to solve problems.

The above idea is not just a dream, but one that begins to operate in some large business corporations; and it suggests how the "world of computers" can help the human family begin to deal more adequately even with evil. Global telecommunications and computer science enable us to reach out to the world's children at risk, and to any other point of injustice, with great power and accuracy. It is as if God is saying, with the advent of high-tech/high-touch technology,[13] "Gather up all the world's children and bring them to me."

So it may be that God is giving his people a new idea of "the end?" Computers are making possible the *completion* of the basic elements of the "mission of the church." The gospel can indeed be proclaimed to all nations – and there is certainly enough food for all if it can be properly distributed. Perhaps even disease and much human suffering can be banished. Some mission thinkers thus speak of "count-down theology." That phrase may be a clue to the direction of theology for the world of computers in a space/information age. And this will be the subject of our final chapter.

PROPHETS OF WHAT GOD IS DOING

Alan Kay, as a child, was on the radio on a national "quiz kid" program. He is also a musician, a rock guitarist who also often disappears to churches to spend hours playing Bach on a pipe organ or to play with jazz groups. The son of an Australian physiologist and a Massachusetts artist, he says that he was always better at sports, guitar playing or "building gizmos" than at conventional school.

A Ph.D in computer science with undergraduate degrees in math and biology, Kay is also well-versed in quantum physics, philosophy, and child psychology. He is one of the most creative people now at work in the world of computers. He is perhaps best known for his "vivarium," a fantastic world he has helped create, a computer-generated learning environment sponsored and funded by the Apple Computer Corporation at the media lab at Massachusetts Institute of Technology and at a primary school in a disadvantaged California neighborhood.

In 1971, when Kay was principal scientist at Xerox PARC, the research center in Palo Alto, he got the vision of the "Dynabook," a simple but powerful computer for school children. He continues to play around with that dream, seeing how education can be significantly reformed and empowered. His Dynabook does not yet exist, although at Apple they are now working on the idea of a computer "Explorer" which any student or researcher could use to explore the wide ranges of human knowledge.

Work on the Dynabook, however, has led to many of most important developments in personal computers. Kay wanted it to be handheld, portable for carrying around. He wanted it to be an art instrument, with a program called "Paint Brush" that children could use to make pictures and *animate* them. He wanted it to allow children to create their own programs and games (this was before the explosion of video games and computer games hit the market). He wanted the Dynabook to link via telephone with the world's libraries, so that each child could have all the world's information at his/her fingertips.

His vivarium is another way to explore and expand the imagination and learning. Kay says that no one "invented" the idea of the vivarium. Like most great creations, it grew from the collaboration of many people. In part, however, it grew from computer experiments Kay and others conducted at primary schools. Many scientists were interested to help children learn, to see what computers could do to enhance their sensitivities and amplify the reach of their learning. Alan Kay also wanted to learn more about children and *how* they grow and develop in creativity.

The vivarium was to enable children to "invent and then unleash realistic organisms in whole 'living' computerized ecologies. This could help them learn about the universe's creation *by doing some of their own.*" In order for it to work, the vivarium needed new kinds of animation and robotics, computer modeling, new and imaginative kinds of "interface" with those who use it – and "possibly a whole new computer architecture" (which might make a highly significant contribution to computer science as a whole). The vivarium idea also needed insights from neurophysiology, ecology, and experimental education; for it offers a way to "organize areas of ignorance into a dramatic whole that invites collaborative assault from usually disparate disciplines."[14]

So the students who continue to create and use the vivarium are creating conceptual software to simulate (to create, in fact) one-celled paramecia and fish. They must deal with the weather, predators, and a total ecological environment. It is a place where children "can hug their tools" (one input device is a kind of teddy bear to play with, squeeze his nose for a menu of things to do, for example) and can create their fantasies. Among the artist/engineer/scientists who have contributed to the vivarium are: a designer of human-powered flying craft, a Disney animator, and a science fiction author.

Since Kay is quite aware of the problems that people often have with computers, he is making sure that the educational aspects of his vivarium are firmly rooted in real life. His children put to work what they learn with the vivarium as they work in a real vegetable garden, and with live animals, as they do their scientific investigation in a real pond.

Kay and some of the vivarium researchers are also highly interested in extending music research with computers so as to include meaning, and "musical compositions which are like living organisms;" interactive music which might end the passive listening that electronic music players have encouraged.

Kay is prepared to help school children use computerized instruments as powerful as a two and one-half million dollar military flight simulator. For example, with the help of a Disney animator and others, two "environments" were put on videodisk. One is an "Infinite Coral Reef" through which any "interactor" could explore under the sea and have a "real" encounter with sharks and all of the magic of that strange world. Instead of just looking at the picture, the participant enters into the picture for learning in an entirely new dimension.

Seeing the vivarium, where scientists are "banging their heads in the playpens of another level of understanding," leads Steward Brand to endorse the idea of bringing science fiction writers to M.I.T. to help create even newer and larger dreams for the scientists to explore. He suggests that creators like Alan Kay, whose work is still at a preliminary stage, may one of these days, for example, enlarge the interconnections of all kinds of technology to model the whole ecology of the planet. They can thus create a total "information health system" to deal with the most complex and sophisticated problems of human society and the economy."

Frank Rose, in an article about Kay entitled "The Pied Piper of the Computer,"[15] says that Alan Kay "figures that in a decade or so, the world will be so tangled up in networks" that without his kind of intelligent agents (computer programs) we will all be helpless. Kay himself, speaking in October, 1988, at the large EDUCOM conference – where university people who work with computers meet – told of his work on a computer in the shape of a helmet which will provide sensual wrap-around simulations where the computer user is "inside" the computer. He said: "The best way to predict the future is to invent it; the best way to help young people learn is to let them construct it."

Thomas Merton (1915–1968) was perhaps the most famous monk of this century. He is a worthy guide, and his life story a worthy topic for reflection as we ask ourselves: What is God doing in the space age? His journey was very significant: it was a journey in ideas, culminating in his Asian trip in which he met the monastic leaders of other faiths, including the Dalai Lama. And it was a geographical journey during which his life ended in Bangkok where he was speaking at the pan-Asian monastic conference.

Merton was an American Trappist monk and writer, a priest in the

Roman Catholic Church (his monastic name was Father Louis) and his Cistercian Abbey of Gethsemani monastery in Kentucky became quite famous.

When Merton was an undergraduate student of English literature at Columbia University, he wanted to be a professional writer and poet. His conversion to Catholicism, his training for the priesthood, and his monastic formation in the order merely delayed the fulfillment of this vocation! Some time after he had settled into his monastic life, a wise Abbot instructed him to write his autobiography. The result was a best-selling exposition of his conversion, *The Seven-Story Mountain* (1948).

As Merton grew in faith and to his spiritual maturity, he wrote many kinds of books and essays, from studies of Zen Buddhism and mysticism (*Mystics and Zen Masters*, 1969) to treatises on ascetical theology (*The Ascent to Truth*) and many poems. He became almost a cult figure in sixties America, and his apologies for the life of the monastery (for example *The Silent Life*) were famous. Some of his writings were both popular and monastic, such as *Contemplative Prayer* and *New Seeds of Contemplation*. Critics evaluate some of his last books as great literature: *Contemplation in a World of Action*, *Conjectures of an Innocent Bystander*, and posthumously his *Asian Journal of Thomas Merton* (1973).

His life of contemplation became a semi-public spiritual pilgrimage which involved him deeply in the interplay of different cultures and spiritual traditions. "In him," Kosuke Koyama said, "the spirituality of the West met that of the East." Even his death was prophetic. He delivered "a radically exiting paper on monasticism and Marxism," Mark Gibbard says, at a pan-monastic conference. It is said that his face was found to be set in "a great and deep peace" when he was accidentally electrocuted by a faulty fan, as if he had found the one for whom he had looked so long and so faithfully. It was as if his death marked a comma or semi-colon in the way his church was digesting the liberating effect of the Second Vatican Council; and similarly the way Christendom as a whole was asking more time to prepare itself for a global vision and spirituality – perhaps one more adequate for this emerging information age.

As we reflect upon Merton's adventurous life, we might ask such questions as these: What can society learn, from the pattern of his experience, about creativity and about what God is doing in the information age? What would be the "ideal monastery" for the information age which might continue his quest, including dialog with non-Christian mystical traditions? What would be the ideal "successor event" to the conference at which Merton died or to the First World Parliament of Religions at which Swami Vivekananda first appeared in America in 1893?

If not at the 1993 World Parliament of Religions, then perhaps at the 2093 World Parliament, scholars will be able to report that "computers and computer networks in dedicated community" are truly helping human beings discover what it can mean to be co-creators with God.

EXERCISES AND PROJECTS

1. *Bible Study*

Isaiah 48: 6–8, "Now I will tell you of new things to come, events that I did not reveal before," could be studied in connection with the *Interpreter's Bible* exegesis and commentary on Isaiah; also see Klaus Koch, *The Prophets*, vol. 2 (London: SCM Press and Philadelphia: Fortress Press, 1983).

2. *Discussion Questions*

(*a*) Do all of God's acts, and all God's self-revelation, lie in the past?

(*b*) If not, how has God acted recently in society and history?

(*c*) What "new things" is God doing now in the world scene? In religion and religions, in science and technology, in politics and the affairs of nations, in the arts, in communications?

(*d*) Discuss whether God is acting in the information age through the phenomena of computer science, A.I., fifth-sixth generation computers, etc.

3. *Theological Reflection*

The Bible reveals God as one who acts in history, who wishes to "do new things," who acts decisively, and – in addition to this – who chooses to explain and reveal himself to "his servants, the prophets." Therefore if God is acting in the information age, God is also seeking to make known his intentions and the meaning of his actions. It is by studying God's previous acts, as in scripture, that we can find the key to what he is doing in the world of computers.

Who then shall listen for God's word of interpretation? Which churches have scientific/well-prepared members standing alert, waiting for that "word" from the Lord?

We should expect to learn more of what God is doing in history now through philosophers of religion (such as John Hick in his books *The Second Christianity* and *God and the Universe of Faiths*). Also, we should look to futurists and all those devout people of all faiths and backgrounds who are possessed of the "prophetic consciousness" – by which we mean a heightened capacity for discerning the presence of God; or in secular terms, the supreme value of righteousness.

The human family today has such prophets in many areas of life; in medicine, for example, Helen Caldicott has campaigned against nuclear weaponry, as Jonathan Schell has in journalism. The prophetic consciousness, the reforming and crusading spirit, the moral imagination and its associated "righteous indignation" are to be found in every type of religious and secular area of civilization.

However, the search for what *God* is doing requires prophets whose passion is for God, whose realm they long to see extended and consummated in the kingdom of shalom/righteousness/justice. Thus Walter Eichrodt, writing in his *Theology of the Old Testament*, speaks of the prophets of Israel as concerned to offer ". . . radical criticism of the contemporary situation on the basis of their new sense of the reality of God."[16] This vision gave real power to Israel ". . . a dynamic power released by a new sense of reality of God" which invaded Israelite life and thought with overwhelming force, sweeping away all that was stagnant to unleash a forward movement which could not be restrained.

The Dominican theologian Edward Schillebeeckx, in a sermon entitled "Jesus the Prophet," shows how the prophetic consciousness is one dominated equally by compassion and a desire for justice. For Schillebeeckx the entire church is also a company of prophets as Christians continue to "proclaim the powerlessness of all human and demonic powers and rules which enslave and oppress men . . ." A prophet, he says, does not repeat the old traditions unimaginatively, but works on tomorrow's new traditions.[17]

Is God today shattering the concept of "local church" in many places to reconstitute it as a network and team of listeners to his word and receivers of his power? Can the parish become a place for controlled experiments relating to spirituality in mission? If so, then worship shifts from what we say to the Lord to what the Lord says to his people who are attentive.

4. *Theological Reading*

Klaus Koch, *The Prophets*, 2 vols. (London: SCM Press, and Philadelphia: Fortress Press, 1980), is a brilliant account of the prophets of Israel as thinkers, who figured out "what God was doing in their age."

5. *Prayers*

Thank you, O God, for shattering our ideas and assumptions, in the world of computers, about "nature" and "natural philosophy," "natural theology," and for showing us that we and our artifacts cannot be arbitrarily separated from earthly materials and substances. Thank you, Lord, for beginning to lead us into a new vision of your own wonderful activities in the information age, and for revealing to us your higher intelligence, your infinitesimal as well as your cosmological attributes, and your presence in the world of technology.

Give to us, O God, a just "theology of technology," based on what you show us of yourself. Break, O God, the frame of our philosophy of technology, and rebuild it around your own divine center, so that henceforward technology goes to the needy and brings them the fruits of your love and goodness – through Christ, our Savior.

Continue, O God, to show us the ways in which the "world of computers" is bringing together in thought and action the religions of the world, so that more alive to your concern for the poor and the lost, the sick and the destitute, the religions repent of their faults and take their place in a just pattern of ministry, through science and technology for the needy.

6. *Meditations*

God is "on the move." The era of nano-technology, with the unbelievable power of computers and their cognate technologies, is God's work. God's inconceivable power and majesty is manifesting itself through "the world of computers." It is God, then, who leads me/us into a deeper grasp of his own nature through the phenomena of the computer world. I/we must wait upon God as we contemplate the wonders of micro-miniaturization and nano-technology, so that progressively God will reveal, to the quiet mind and the penitent spirit, the meaning of these new revelations of his own might, omnipresence, "collective intelligence," infinite speed.

Thanks be to God, who in the phenomena of the world of computers is shattering our concepts of his previous revelations, and who is giving us in this way a whole new foundation for our understanding of God's self-revelation – its content and its history. Thank you, Lord, for revealing to us, in the quasi-nature of technology, new facets of your own boundless being, and for initiating the human race into a higher relationship with the limitless range and scope, the intelligence and relatedness, of the divine life.

And thank you, Lord, for the leaders whom you are now raising up to decode for us this new revelation, so that it can be made available to heal the sick, to end unnecessary suffering, and to save the poor and helpless, your own people on this, your world.

7. *Worship Suggestions*

Call to worship: Selected from meditation above.

Bible study on the Lord "doing a new thing," Isaiah 43:19.

Presentations of news of "prophets" who have spoken out on computer science.

Talk on the possibilities of a "prophetical guild" (2 Kings 2) of prophets within the world of information technology and global telecommunications.

Gospel: John 14:12 ("greater things than this you can do").

Sermon.

Offertory of each participant's understanding of what God is doing in the information age.

Holy Communion to consecrate the resultant intentions and insights.

Post-worship *evaluation* of the integrity and productivity of the worship experience.

8. *Further Reading*

Stuart Blanch, *For All Mankind*, a popular introduction to the Old Testament and a useful entry point for thinking about the prophets.

Mark Gibbard, *Twentieth Century Men of Prayer* (London: SCM Press, 1975).

Cheslyn Jones et al, eds., *The Study of Spirituality* (London: SPCK, 1986), a massive but indispensable six hundred page anthology.

Eberhard Bethge, *Dietrich Bonhoeffer* (London: Collins, and New York: Harper and Row, 1970).

NOTES

1. Frank Rose, "Pied Piper of the Computer," *New York Times Magazine* (Oct. 8, 1987).

2. In a brilliant but neglected treatise, *Civilization, Science and Religion* (1945).

3. Prof. Lochhead of the University of British Columbia is preparing to publish a theological book on diskette and on a computer network where others may comment on it and suggest revisions.

4. See Walter T. Anderson's *To Govern Evolution*, which shows that there is now no turning back.

5. Those who wish to study more about the covenant concept of religion should see Eichrodt's *Theology of the Old Testament*, Vol. 1 (London: SCM Press, and Philadelphia: The Westminster Press, 1971).

6. See the chapter on Piaget in J. K. Radford and A. Burton, *Thinking* (New York: Wiley, 1974).

7. See Glynn Harmon, "Toward Encyclopedic Intelligence," *Bulletin of the American Society for Information Science* (Oct./Nov. 1988).

8. *Op. cit.*, 26.

9. Some hope that this can be the achievement of the Centennial World Parliament of Religions in 1993.

10. Psychologically speaking, it is well known that the "ego defense mechanism" of denial can lead persons not only to disown responsibility for their own actions and their own possessions, but to run for their lives far away from the scene of their obligations, forgetting that wherever they go their own self goes with them. See Gordon Arthur, "Child Theology," *Global Visions* (vol. 1, no. 1, 1990).

12. "Creating a Corporate Brain," *Bulletin of the American Society for Information Science* (Oct./Nov. 1988).

13. The terminology of Naisbitt in *Megatrends* (New York: Warner, 1982).

14. These quotations are from Stewart Brand, *The Media Lab: Inventing the Future at M.I.T.* (New York: Viking Press, 1987).

15. *New York Times Magazine* (Oct. 8, 1977).

16. Walter Eichrodt, *Theology of the Old Testament*, Vol. 1, (London: SCM Press, and Philadelphia: The Westminster Press, 1961), 387.

17. Edward Schillebeeckx, *God Among Us* (London: SCM Press and New York: Crossroad Publishing Co, 1982), 33–44.

9

Christian Life
in the Information Age

We have been tempted to talk about a "new theology" – since God speaks of "making all things new." However, some scholar or other is always proposing a theology that is supposed to be new, generally without much significant response. Perhaps a genius will arise, another Aquinas, with a theological vision large enough to take account of the complexity of the emerging space/information age.

We suspect, however, that the needed new vision which will integrate the vast discoveries of modern science with a larger and more powerful and compassionate religious perspective will not be achieved by any one genius. That will require the bringing together of many minds – a global team of theologians and scientists who can use computer-powered "collective intelligence" so that many minds can accomplish together what is no longer possible for one mind alone.

Now as we conclude, however, we summarize by saying that the changes reviewed in the previous chapters suggest something new about what it means to be the people of God in the world of computers, which is such a crucial center of the emerging information age.

We have hinted from time to time about prospects for a "theology of science,"even about a "scientific theology." However, it might make more sense to talk about an "experimental theology" for a scientific age and milieu – a theology of adventure (as in space travel). What we really want to suggest is an entirely new approach to "proving the truth of the Christian faith" or of any other religion, for that matter. Christians have often been accused of having a religion of the head, rather than of the heart, seeing religion (even agape = love) as something to argue about rather than something first to live. The only real proof of Christianity comes only to those who sacrificially give their lives in loving service for others, the truth being revealed thus only on the cross.

So the title of this chapter is not "Christian theology" or "Christian ideas," but "Christian life" for the world of computers and the information age.

It is almost impossible for theologians to keep up with all that is going on in science; indeed few scientists can even keep up with their own field. We might wish and hope for an "information age theology" which would integrate all of the findings of the best science. What we propose for the world of computers, however, is an "experimental theology" which shifts the meaning of the "Christ event" in history away from what we believe or feel about it to what we *do* lovingly *for others*.

Jesus was very clear about this: His "way" is love of God and neighbor (neighbor defined as those who most need help), and those who wish to find and serve Christ (to find and share in his kingdom of love) will find him through serving those who are sick, hungry, in prison, and so forth. We have all known people who are cruel and heartless yet who claim to "have been saved." Isn't Michael Goulder right when he says: "To be saved is to love?"

We can summarize the faith and life needed in the computer world under successive headings: *summum bonum*, religion, theology, science, church.

The Summum Bonum

Those who live and work in the world of computers, dominating the information age, need a clearer idea of the *summum bonum* (supreme or highest good). What, indeed, is worth dying for?

The *highest good* in the information age, we suggest, especially since humanity now has the scientific knowledge and skill to make it possible, is the liberation *of the entire human race* from bondage to poverty, disease, and social injustice. The problem is the political will, the faith and motivation, the compassion to do so. Theology/politics is the search for the governance of the world (including and beginning with the world of computers) in such a way as to achieve this end. (For Christians: the kingdom of God; for Muslims: Sharia; etc.)

The highest good that has been revealed to humanity so far is the "healing" and redemption of the entire population of this planet (six billion in all – and indeed also the healing of "Gaia," the ecological system of the increasingly polluted planet itself.

Justice for all, or however you may wish to sum up the highest good, is the subject matter of theology, politics, and computer science alike. It is the next step and destiny of the political order and of all authentically human organizations and communities, whatever the next centuries may unfold of God's will once such justice is accomplished. We suspect that after justice, the next calling will be to creativity and the discovery and fulfillment of the human potential of every individual and community in the world.

Meanwhile, this next step (justice for all) requires a new synthesis of *critical intelligence*, where many scientists and artificial intelligence specialists are strong, and *empathic outreaching love*. It should involve a veritable revolution in the whole field of knowledge: a revolution of goodness, not of violence; and it also requires an "about turn" in our thinking about "human destiny."

Supposing that this revolution is indeed going on, bringing heart and mind together, how can the people of God take part in it? It is our thesis that religious and scientific leaders need to work together to develop an integrated, compassionate science and technology. In computer science this can lead, we have suggested, to new products, new methods, new philosophy, amid a new supportive community. In religious words, it is at once a prophetic, a priestly, and a political task. It should remind us of what was said about William Pitt the Elder, who became the Earl of Chatham: he was a statesman who had the ability "to get the State moving."

Love and care for our planet – to reverse the destruction of ecology – and love and care for all its children, requires more than the best science (though that is terribly important). It requires powerful motivation – the faith and will as well as the thought – "to get things moving."

Once this vision of the integration of computerized technology and compassion is grasped by a few, we can imagine it spreading like a contagion of goodness, like wildfire through the computer-assisted hyperwebs of today and tomorrow. That would be good news indeed, an "anti-type" to the malignant "programming viruses" which some computer "hackers" have been planting in software in the hope of creating a chain reaction of destruction within computer networks.

Maybe this is an unrealistic image: the expanding power of goodness migrating from computer group to computer group, bequeathing hope, compassion, and spiritual power as it passes on its electronic way among multi-media pathways. These electronic networks, however, have been accurately described as the "highways of tomorrow" which are uniting the earthwide human community. How else can any kind of vision of the highest good be spread to all except along the paths which people will be following?

Experimental Religion and Spirituality

We speak now of "religion," not just of Christianity, for we now live in a global community where all the world's religions meet and enter more and more into dialogue. Increasingly, people in the different religious communities must listen to one another, understand one another, learn from one another, and will inevitably challenge one another.

When people of different religions meet in conference – as they will at the 1993 World Parliament of Religions – it is usually to talk about what they believe and where they disagree, which of course is useful for mutual understanding. We suggest, however, a more "experimental" approach to each other, a testing of faith. For example, the World Network of Religious Futurists set up its first major conference to be such a challenge, asking a representative of each major world religion what it was doing for the world's hungry children; and what that religion might do better to accomplish such justice.

In other words, can the different religions challenge each other in a competition to see who can show the most compassion? How can motivation to act in this way be increased?

Now of course if the religious communities undertake "experiments," these need not be a quest for "hybrid" religions or "syncretism." We propose, instead, a joint search for how love and compassion can better be nurtured in all people and communities. Each religion has more depth than this, but each can prove that it is more than this by seeking ways to use and combine the spiritual power of all "to get things moving" in the solving of humanity's and the earth's most fundamental problems.

We have seen Jews, Buddhists, Muslims, and Christians walking side by side in protests against acid rain and in peace marches, for example. Each can remember with appreciation how Buddha invited the people of ancient India to join him individually and collectively in the *Sangha*, the community of Buddhist monks, on a journey to Nirvana, the place of peace. And Christ Jesus summoned all to follow him on a similar journey, a journey of repentance which could lead to the love of God. So can scientific (experimentally minded) religious futurists of today also invite people all over the world – and in outer space too as humans go there – on a journey to discover and nurture love and peace? Can all be equipped with a new weave of compassionate science and experimental and intelligent religion?

It seems to us that a life style linking computers with compassion is a road, a path, along which the human race must now walk. Only then can the emerging powerful new technology (which can remake human beings, which can explore the stars, which can empower and transform human science and thought) be used for human survival and for a richer human life rather than for destruction.

One group of young Christians (the Community of Saint John, which is dedicated to science) seeks to live according to an "information age" recasting of the Noble Eightfold Path of Buddhism. It is reported below. They propose a twenty-first century equivalent of the "Noble Eightfold Path" as something first of all for scientists, but also then for children and teenagers and old people as well as the rest of humanity. They envisage it as a way to peace and justice for all, as the "experimental religion," as proposed above, results in an outreach to all suffering creatures, thanks to the dramatically potent and incredibly rapid apparatus now available to us in technology.

This proposal is but one hint of what religious "experimenting" might become. Alfred North Whitehead spoke of "religion in the making," which suggests to us many more experiments in religion as well as in technology and science. For we are perhaps now entering an era of experimental religion, empowered for example by the capacity of computer technology to collect and compare more hundreds of thousands of case studies of religious experience than has ever before been possible.

Science

What can religious people say to the scientific community, such as the world of computers, that has not already been said and "yawned over" before? Beyond "philosophies of science"[1] and theologies of science, a group of dedicated computer people have covenanted together in the "Community of St John" to follow "The Eightfold Way of the Sacred Scientist." They hope it will be the "path of knowledge/life/community" of an emerging community of "sacred scientists." What that means is clarified below in the summary of their "way."

Their document begins with the suggestion that viewers of *Star Trek* are familiar with: the idea of a sudden surge forward into warp speed, a higher dimension of acceleration and motion and journeying. This is a metaphor for what some young scientists hope will be a result of a "new mixture of science and religion, as both these stands of culture curve in towards the great mass of human suffering."

As we mentioned earlier, Siddartha Gautama, known as the Buddha or the Enlightened One, proclaimed his Noble Eightfold Path – the way to Nirvana or Peace – some two and a half millennia ago. Its eight steps form the basis of Buddhism along with Four Noble Truths and three pillars of religion. The eight steps are often described as "right" knowledge, work, speech, meditation, etc. They are ways for any individual person to find peace.

The "Way of the Sacred Scientist" follows that outline, adding the Christian concern for all persons, for all of society, and especially the deprived, tormented, etc., as seen below:

(1) *Right Prayer*, a surprising definition, is "fully grown-up[2] thinking." It is to place God, God's wholeness, truth and love, at the center of one's thoughts.

(2) *Right Relationship* as a religious principle and life style for the scientific community, suggests that life is made up neither of independence nor dependence, but interdependence. In right relationships we seek always to share ourselves with our colleagues and companions along the way, building up one another's and the group's capacity to discover truths which can reduce human and animal suffering. "Right relationship" is not manipulative or dishonest, but open, searching, authentic and encouraging, a life style which produces good works for all of humanity. It celebrates, respects and helps other people: ". . . intelligent and productive collaboration is the sign that of right relationship."

(3) *Right Theology*, for scientists of the "way," "is anti-religious, anti-pious." It is the enemy of idolatry of all kinds, especially that insidious ideology which makes theology itself the object of religious concerns to the exclusion of God and neighbor. Right theology is reflection on the relationships between God's power and the needs of the neglected. Thus "a powder keg of conceptual explosive . . . is everywhere bursting into a holy fire of enthusiasm for outreach to the lost and neglected creatures of the cosmos." It is "discovering, naming, locating, and going to the needy with the power of the living God and the instruments which he provides."

(4) *Right Direction* in sacred science is "towards the diminution of human suffering and injustice, and the improvement of the cultural ideals and realities of the human family. If our sciences and technologies are not headed that way, they are going in the wrong direction and need to be developed in a higher moral synthesis."

(5) *Right Science* "is the quest for knowledge which builds the kingdom of God . . .," "God-centered knowing, thinking and investigating." Right science thus involves an "ongoing ethical and moral appraisal of the nature, aims and methods of science, the scientific

outlook . . ." And each individual scientist should "be monitoring his or her own field of science . . . noting ethical horizons." Right science is also engaging in research in one's field of expertise, "knowing its strengths and weaknesses." It includes right knowing and attention to God which is shared with others in the context of worship or corporate spirituality.

(6) *Right Acceleration* is the willed effort to hasten progress in the diminution of human misery, "an extension of the gospel into time itself," the "constant discussion of means by which the pace of moral-scientific progress can be accelerated towards the destination of every individual vector of moral-scientific achievement."

(7) *Right Technology* is "scientific insight in action," knowledge made tangible. "The enemy of right technology is not so much wrong technology as 'laziness'! Right technologies are also those which have been designed for the amelioration of suffering and building the best possible human society."

(8) *Right Creativity* is the "constant alertness of the individual and the group for breakthrough of any and every kind in the ideas and realities of scred science itself." It is prayerfully seeking new inspiration about creativity itself, and thus is the "crest-jewel" of this path – its lotus bloom in which the potential of the previous seven steps rays out into "glorious fulfilment."

As Stapledon says in the conclusion to *Last and First Men*, human beings themselves are music, at the very least, "a brave music that also makes of its vast accompaniment, its matrix of storms and stars." So also the scientist is a *composer* and scientists need "to help each other evaluate and progressively refine and potentiate their products, compositions, inventions."

Experimental Theology

A theology of compassion is tested by its success in accomplishing, for example, what Jesus proposed (demanded?) in the parable of The Last Judgment (I was hungry and you did not feed me, I was sick and in prison and you did not come unto me). Traditionally the "prolegomena" to theology have to do with the conceptual elements of philosophy, the challenge of intellectual ideas. By the test of compassion, however, the "prolegomena" of theology are the facts of "world pain," the plight of the world's children, the political tyranny that supports injustice and the ecological pollution, degradation and other needs and hungers to be addressed by theology and the people of God.

William Nicholls in the *Pelican Guide to Modern Theology* tells how Paul Tillich, this century's "theologian of culture," sought to recast the theology of his time to help people find the aspect of the gospel which is relevant to this age:

People in the *early days* of the church were preoccupied with death so theologians focused on immortality and union with God.

People in the *Middle Ages* were preoccupied with guilt, so the reforming theologians focused on the grace of God, and justification by grace through faith.

People in the *modern age*, Tillich saw, have been most concerned with the contradictions and estrangements which have come into modern life. So he proposed that theology should focus on "New Being" in Jesus Christ.

People in the *emerging information age* now require a different theological starting point. We can agree with Tillich's brilliant analyses of the successive concerns of humankind in the great epochs of history – for theology has its aeons as much as geology. But the human race today, a century after Tillich's childhood, is now overwhelmed by, and sometimes even obsessed by, technology. It is often seen as depersonalizing, and as having the potential to destroy the human community and even the earth itself. If we fear death as people in the early days of the church, and if we have guilt as people in the Middle Ages, we now also confront the potential death of the planet and a nagging guilt over the sickness (as seen in the faces of all those starving children) of our human community itself.

Our starting point for theology is this: *Where is my neighbor? What is his/her need?* And secondly: *How can computer-empowered "collective intelligence" be used for and in theology by the people of God?*[3]

This suggests dramatic changes in the focus of theology. On the one side, its subject matter becomes "our neighbor,"[4] see Matthew 25:31–44. On the other hand, its method moves from the individual theologian's efforts to produce or refine doctrines, to groups of theologians (and scientists and plain Christians) seeking together to find and to love their worldwide neighbors – concurrently seeking and finding the power of God to do so.[5]

We propose the term "vector theology" as a framework for summing up what has been discussed here, and as a way to seek answers to some information/computer age provocative questions:

– Can theology have a mission to each science and each technology?

– Can theology have a mission to scientific method itself?

– What are the lessons which theology can learn from science in its conceptual apparatus and its instruments of discovery and communication?

– What theological elements exist within the history of modern science itself?

– What might be the role of each major science in advancing the religious causes of love and justice in the world?

– What is the contribution of the sciences – content, methods and community – to missiology in all its dimensions?

Vector theology implies an experimental theology (in the sense that sciences undertake experiments) in its own right. It seeks to bring under the theological canopy all of the important questions and discoveries of modern science that have bearing on human nature (biology, mind research, for example), God's creation (astronomy and relativity theory, for example), and so forth. It is oriented towards the acceleration of that scientific discovery which catalyzes the values of the parable of The Last Judgment (feeding the world's hungry, for example) in Matthew 25.

It proposes an ecclesiology which transforms the theology of the local church, the congregation, towards the "model" of an experimental research unit (laboratory, workshop, think tank). It experiments with translating love and compassion into realistic action, seeking the power by which mission is generated, sustained, and consummated.[6]

Vector theology seeks to turn the attention of theologians (and all Christians) to mission, as Newbigin defines a mission to contemporary science and culture. Where "process theology" seeks to move from substance to process, we see vector theology as moving a stage further from process to direction. We are using vector to mean "force plus direction" (and acceleration). The force is love, the direction is God's will for "the least of these" to be consummated by God's grace working through the people of God on earth.

Theology and Collective Intelligence in the Future

Theology, of course, has always been a collective enterprise. Giants like Augustine, Aquinas, Buber, or Barth have built upon the work of countless other scholars, known or unknown. They debated their ideas with students and colleagues, testing and enlarging concepts as ideas and systems grew.

In the information/computer age, however, theologians *can work together more effectively*, as befits Christian community. If we consider a major gift of the gospel to be the abolition of barriers between people, then a gift of the gospel to tomorrow's theology is a summons to a more responsible and shared collective enterprise, in which seeking and finding is more deeply shared.

Should not all theological schools and scholars, for example, assume a share of the task of putting the history of theology, the entire tradition, into (electronic computerized) hypertext so that anyone – scholar, student, scientist or interested person – could easily journey through the entire corpus of tradition . . . as students at Brown University do in English literature? That task would enable clearer definitions of disagreements and areas where more study, reflection, and research are needed. That could provide a foundation for larger joint projects in which theologians all over the world would divide tasks up and coordinate their efforts in more comprehensive and "wholistic" research.

Theologians can function according to parallel and not serial processing (computer terms). With computer-assisted parallel processing, theologians-in-community (residential or computer-network-assisted communities of scholars scattered all over the world) can simultaneously bring many minds together to work on one idea or project. Many related interdisciplinary projects could also be simultaneously addressed.

Science/theology practiced this way is truly "collective intelligence" (using computer empowerment tools to help people think and work together more effectively). This, we suggest, can be the religious counterpart to "artificial intelligence" (computers doing people's thinking for them). The fusing of expertise through networks of minds can result in dozens (and later thousands) of interconnected "computer nth generation" scholars working simultaneously on different aspects of the same problem.

Future (electronic and continuously updated) theological journals, for example, can take one important idea or problem and deal with it intensively, year after year, drawing upon top minds all over the world to define each point of disagreement, every possibility for illumination, to see how far theological thought can be enriched in that area; and the same applies to "applied theological" issues, such as the solution of ecological or population problems.

Not only theologians, but also congregations, can develop and employ such "collective intelligence." Each local church can thus become part of a more and more resourceful web of self-help support networks, as well as being an "experimental laboratory" in mission.

Thus theology, with the world of computers, can enter into an era of more responsible and adequate collective intelligence. Such collective theology – creative people working together – can result in "synergy," the emergent whole which is greater than the sum of the separate parts (reported from time to time in computer literature).

Theology "on-line" (published and daily updated on computer networks, data bases, and bulletin boards) can deliver the church from "authoritarian" religion – in which ideas are "frozen" in print – and can initiate it into responsibly experimental religion.

We suggest that such collective intelligence in theology can also promote creativity as it helps us to think in new and more powerful ways, combining elements of memory and reflection which have been difficult to integrate before.

As minds are aided electronically to reach out to other minds with empowered creativity – and the global telephone system has already demonstrated this in limited ways – bursts of spiritual imagination can be directed to the completion of "the great unfinished agenda"[7] which Christ laid before the human race. The coming of age of computer-empowered collective intelligence can be of tremendous significance, moral and political, as well as religious. Therefore it should become a high priority as religious leaders dialogue with scientists and politicians.

As we near the end of this conversation with our readers, we summarize the demands and the hope of Christian life in the information age. The central demand is that henceforward computers and their industry, through the radical partnership of science and religion/theology, may be used for justice and human service, to ensure sustenance and freedom for every human creature.

LIFE STYLE PROPHETS

Nicolas Negroponte, director of the Media Lab at Massachusetts Institute of Technology, is a real genius and creator in the world of computers, aware that he is leading the world into a profound transition in which, he says, monologues become conversations; the impersonal becomes personal; and the traditional "mass media" will essentially disappear.

Negroponte, however, is a "business executive type" who according to *Fortune* magazine looks more like a matinee idol. He comes from an old Greek shipping family and grew up in Switzerland. He is always beautifully groomed and dressed, and some of his genius is in raising millions of dollars to fund exciting projects at M.I.T. from corporate leaders who rightly see him as "one of the inventors of the future."

He is so oriented to computer instruments and networks that he works each day with his staff at M.I.T., via computer networks, even if he is in Japan or Europe. He lives his vision that computers are bringing all technologies together in a "joint metamorphosis." As all media are digitalized, they all come together, changing each other, breeding, enlarging, interacting.

For a while, Negroponte worked at the World Computer Center in Paris. Its founders had the dream of using powerful computer technology for Third World development, to redress the balance of wealth and services between the rich and poor. When Negroponte came from Paris to M.I.T. he set out to provide the resources for an unusually creative team of scientists to work on art, music, childhood education, new forms of interactive media and entertainment (to empower ordinary people to control their own lives and learning). His concern for human-computer interface, and more creative and powerful computer architecture, is motivated by a passionate concern for improving the quality of human life, as well as making it possible for corporations to make money by creating and selling products to do so.

Regardless of the man-machine relationship, he says, the goal must be a better human life for all. In his own life style he cherishes individual eccentricity and freedom, Stewart Brand says, in describing how Negroponte works electronically while wandering informally around his home. In different words, Negroponte's life and work reflect the observations of one sage: that when a person really finds his or her *calling* in life, the work is so enjoyable that work and play become inseparable, and one could be happy to do the work even if one did not need pay for it.

Negroponte is especially incensed about "unethical robots." Yet he points out that we are as yet far from having ethical human beings! So the designing of ethical robots is going to be a long hard process, and it may help humans become more ethical along the way; just as experimentation with artificial intelligence – with understanding how people think – may help people think better.

Negroponte, still young, dreams of "personalizing and deeply humanizing absolutely everything."

Pierre Teilhard de Chardin, S.J. (1861–1955), was a French scientist and Jesuit priest. By profession he was a paleontologist. He won great acclaim after his death when his previously suppressed books were published. Many, though not all, eminent scientists and theologians acclaimed him as a great philosopher of evolution, and a pioneer of the first rank in the harmonization of science and religion. However, other scientists, such as the late Sir Peter Medawar, considered him not to be a very good scientist.

His contribution to paleontology, and his priestly reflections on his observations of the animal ancestry of man (and evolution), led him to write several now-famous treatises: *The Phenomenon of Man*, *The Future of Man*, and *The Divine Milieu*. Perhaps not without irony we can report that today his reputation is probably higher among scientists (even "atheists" such as Julian Huxley, author of *Religion Without Revelation*) than among theologians. For example, the two astronomers, John Barrow and Frank Tipler, authors of *The Anthropic Cosmological Principle*, speak enthusiastically of him: "Teilhard combined in one person the scientist and theologian: he had acquired a worldwide reputation as a paleontologist specializing in the evolution of Man; he also was a Jesuit priest. When it came to reconciling science and religion, as a scientist and theologian, he could speak with double authority" (New York: Oxford, 1988), 196.

Theologians tend to see Teilhard as a visionary, a kind of mystical poet-biologist, an amateur in theology as he was professional in biological science. Much of the legend of Teilhard seems to have arisen because he was apparently a "martyr." His books and thoughts were long suppressed by the Jesuit leaders of his time. So he became a geographical and ecclesiastical exile, dying in America, not his native France.

Teilhard was a genuine innovator in the world of ideas, although whether those ideas are biological or theological is difficult to say. Perhaps he is best considered as a biologist who speculated on the future of species. He might then be classified as a futurist/anthropologist. His mystical propensities lent a vaguely Christian cast to his thinking, but his was not a vision rooted in the biblical ethos. It owes more perhaps to Charles Darwin. His deepest significance lies in the fact that he encouraged biologists and cosmologists to think about a "melioristic cosmos" and its destiny.

Theologians also complain that there is scant attention to sin and evil in his vision. Like Olaf Stapledon (see our chapter 6), Teilhard's "hero" is Man (humanity), not men. His talent as an archetypal "ideas man" allowed him to dream of the final Omega Point – an idea now often embraced by cosmologists – a time when God will be all in all. He enriched the vocabulary of mysticism with other ideas such as the "Noosphere" or intellectual atmosphere of this planet: ". . . an awakening of thought . . . (which) marks a transformation affecting the state of the entire planet. We have the beginning of a new age," he said, as "the earth finds its soul."

Teilhard is important in the history of science/religion relationships because he helped, and continues to help scientists to discover some of their deeper ethical feelings. Looking at his life we can ask what kind of figure would allow scientists, (for example, those in the world of computers) to discover their deeper feelings about sin, evil, and their redemption. As we reflect upon the life of Teilhard de Chardin we could also ask such questions as: Can one live a life true to God while embracing the deepest values of scientific Darwinism? Do scientists need to give more serious consideration to the reality of good and evil . . . if they are biologists and/or cosmologists? What would be the ultimate concerns of a "sacred scientist" like Teilhard, but with a deeper commitment to the biblical revelation and a concomitant loyalty to the Holy Spirit and the church?

Teilhard's life was relatively straightforward, with Jesuit training interrrupted by service as a stretcher-bearer in France during the First World War. He died in New York City on Easter Sunday, 1955. He saw love to be energy, a general property of all life, as a "ray of light" to help us see and understand all that is around us. "Love," he said, is alone capable of uniting human beings in such a way as to complete and fulfil them. "A universal love . . . is the only complete and final way in which we are able to love" (*The Phenomenon of Man*, London: Collins and New York: Harper Torchbooks, 1959, pp. 265–67).

Thomas Forsyth Torrance was challenged in the 1960s by the eminent astronomer, Sir Bernard Lovell, to define the sense or senses in which Christian theology could claim to be scientific. Torrance's key idea, in his writings and research ever since, has been "theology and science learning from one another."

Torrance was born in 1913 at Chengdu, Sichuan, China, the eldest son of Scottish missionaries, the Rev. Thomas and Annie E. Torrance. He attended school in China until he was fourteen and went to Scotland to continue his education there. Education has been a central experience in his life. He began his university studies at Edinburgh where he received an M.A. in Classical Languages and Philosophy. In 1937, three years later, he also took his B.D. degree at Edinburgh in Systematic Theology.

The war years interrupted, or marked a semicolon in his studies, and it was not until 1946 that the now-ordained Church of Scotland pastor and ex-Army Chaplain took his doctorate in Switzerland. At the University of Basel his doctoral thesis was on the doctrine of grace in the Apostolic Fathers, thus revealing his lifelong conviction of the importance of the patristic period for truth in Christian theology.

He was then almost immediately invited to America to become Professor of Systematic Theology at Auburn Theological Seminary in New York. This early appointment both confirmed his precocity and prefigured a lifetime's collaboration with American institutions which culminated, perhaps, in his contribution to the creation of the Center for Theological Inquiry (for dialogue between scientists and theologians) at Princeton in the 1980s.

When Torrance received the prestigious Templeton Prize for Progress in Religion in 1978, it was a notable tribute to his sixty-fifth birthday, which he celebrated as Professor of Christian Dogmatics at the University of Edinburgh. The previous year this apostle of "theological science" had crowned an illustrious career by serving as Moderator of the General Assembly of the Church of Scotland.

Of all living theologians, T. F. Torrance has probably done most to promote the deep integration of what he calls "natural science and theological science." After his challenge from astronomer Lovell, Torrance wrote his 1968 volume, *Theological Science* – dedicated to Lovell – and a number of later volumes such as *Reality and Scientific Theology* (1985), which was itself part of a series edited by Torrance: *Theology and Science at the Frontiers of Knowledge.*

In 1980, in *Christian Theology and Scientific Culture*, he wrote: "Christian theology (must be prepared to) engage in radical and critical clarification of its own conceptual tradition in light of questions arising from its intersection with scientific developments." By doing this, Christianity can contribute creatively to the "controlling ideas of this scientific culture."[8]

The academic theologian has been a prolific writer as well as a much-respected teacher. Nearly five hundred publications are credited to him in his voluminous bibliography, including over thirty books. The many series of lectures he has given have taken him to New York and Dundee, Connecticut (Yale), Mississippi and Montreal, Virginia,

Belfast and Pasadena, California. He also founded the Society for the Study of Theology in the U.K. in 1952 and served as its president, 1956–68.

This theologian also found time to be a family man with a long and happy marriage. He and his wife, Margaret, have raised their children, including a new generation of theologians, in addition to a period of service as a parish minister at Alyth, Perthshire; and army service which led to his being awarded the M.B.E.

Torrance has been a leading figure in ecumenical dialog and has provided several volumes of theory to support this, in such books as *Theology in Reconciliation* (1975). Because of his works on Karl Barth, under whom he studied at Basel, and who invited Torrance to revise his works, Thomas Torrance has been described as the leading interpreter of the famous Swiss theologian.

What, then, has Torrance contributed to theology's dialog with the "world of computers"? It has not been to "do theological experiments." It has not been to redeem the world of science or to challenge the very trajectory of computer science or mathematics. Instead it has been to "model or embody the life of a theologian in the world of science," in his own sense a "scientific theologian." This has not, we should point out, consisted of a theologian living out his life in a kind of theological laboratory, or even a scientific one. He has not become famous as a theologian using telescopes or polygraphs. His writings have remained within the traditional format of doctrinal theology. He has not become "scientific" in the sense of publishing data based on hypthetico-deductive scientific research.

Instead, he has written his traditional theology in such a way as to show a profound familiarity with and a great respect for the world of scientific thought, especially theoretical physics.

The result, in part, is perhaps that which is often the fate of "bridge-builders:" falling between stools, or pleasing neither party. *Scientists* might feel that his "science" remains art, or humanities-based doctrine. *Theologians*, or simply practicing Christians, might offer the opposite criticism: that so far from *endorsing* such scientists as Einstein, Christians should be refounding physics on the gospel of God. But such criticism may perhaps be asking too much of a pioneer such as Torrance . . . especially in a time when the first task is simply to open conversations between scientists and theologians.

Thus there may be disagreement with his understanding of science, and his program of "theological science," but his life and work is an inspiring example of a contemporary thinker who has inhabited the respectable center of church and society; yet who at the same time has sought to live on the edges of thought: at the "frontiers" of science and theology.

Christians "in the world of computers" may want their theology and their science to be profoundly more experimental, their research to be deeply shared and collaborative – exhibiting what we have called "collective intelligence." But we end with a tribute to Torrance whose work stands firm as a "launching pad," ready to receive the thrust of "theological" computer science and not to collapse under the energies it is to receive. His "theological science" is a true beginning and he is the only major theologian we have found who is exploring the possibility of getting his life's work onto a major "computerized data base" so that students and scholars in the future may continue to build upon his work and expand it.

In the book, *Levitating Trains and Kamikaze Genes: Technological Literacy for the 1990s* (New York: Wiley, 1990), Richard Berman presents evidence that you and I have little hope of coping with the increasingly rapid changes in society . . . medicine, outer space, the environment, etc., unless we become much better informed about technology that is increasingly interconnected and powered by computers.

Have you decided to remain content in the previous age?

NOTES

1. See T. F. Torrance, *Transformation and Convergence in the Frame of Knowledge* (Belfast: Christian Journals, Ltd., 1984).

2. These definitions are taken from "The Situation of the Sacred Scientists" (London: Order of the Academy of Christ, 1988).

3. See Parker Rossman, "Theology and Collective Intelligence in the Future," *Visions* (Sept. 1986, vol. 4, no. 3).

4. Homer A. Jack, ed., *World Religion and World Peace* (Boston: Beacon Press, 1968), 182–83.

5. For biblical teachings on love of neighbor, see Genesis 4:3; Luke 10:25–37.

6. See Tillich, *Systematic Theology*, three phases of God's activity.

7. See chapter 6 in Rossman, *Computers: Bridges to the Future*.

8. These quotations are both from *Christianity and Scientific Culture* (Belfast: Christian Journals, Ltd, 1980), 14.

Index